SPARKNOTES™

5 Practice Tests for the SAT II Writing

2003 Edition

Editorial Director Justin Kestler

Executive Editor Ben Florman

Managing Editor Vince Janoski

Technical Director Tammy Hepps

Series Editor John Crowther

Editor Nile Lanning

Contributing Editor Jen Chu

SPARKNOTES is a registered trademark of SparkNotes LLC.

This edition published by Spark Publishing.

Spark Publishing
A Division of SparkNotes LLC
120 Fifth Avenue, 8th Floor
New York, NY 10011

Please submit all comments and questions or report errors to www.sparknotes.com/errors

Library of Congress information available upon request

Printed and bound in Canada

ISBN 1-58663-873-4

SparkNotes is neither affiliated with nor endorsed by Harvard University.

Welcome to SparkNotes Test Preparation

IF YOU WANT TO SCORE HIGH ON THE SAT II WRITING, YOU NEED TO KNOW more than just the material—you need to know how to take the test. Practice tests are the most effective method for learning the ins and outs of the test. But practice tests that accurately reflect the actual SAT II Writing have been hard to find—until now. *5 More Practice Tests for the SAT II Writing* is the first book anywhere dedicated to giving you accurate practice tests so you can perfect your test-taking skills. This book contains:

- **Five full-length SAT II Writing tests.** The practice tests in this book are the most accurate, true-to-life tests available. Our experts, who've been teaching the SAT II Writing for years, researched the exam extensively so they could give you tests that reflect exactly what you'll see at the test center. Our tests replicate the format and content of the actual test so closely that nothing will catch you off guard on test day.

- **Clear, helpful explanations for every question—so you can study smarter.** Our explanations do more than tell you the right answer—they identify flaws in your thinking and show you exactly what topics you need to work on. We help you pinpoint your weaknesses, so you can make your studying more efficient by going straight to the stuff you need to review.

- **Specific, proven strategies for the SAT II Writing.** We give you smart, easy strategies on the best ways to guess, pace yourself, and find shortcuts to answers. These strategies help you maximize your score by showing you how to avoid the test's traps and turn the test's format to your own advantage.

Contents

Orientation

Practice Tests

Orientation

Introduction to the SAT II Tests

THE SAT II SUBJECT TESTS are created and administered by the College Board and the Educational Testing Service (ETS), the two organizations responsible for producing the dreaded SAT I (which most people call the SAT). The SAT II Subject Tests were created to act as complements to the SAT I. Whereas the SAT I tests your critical thinking skills by asking math and verbal questions, the SAT II Subject Tests examine your knowledge of particular subjects, such as writing, U.S. history, physics, and biology. The SAT I takes three hours; the Subject Tests take only one hour.

In our opinion, the SAT II Subject Tests are better tests than the SAT I because they cover definitive topics rather than some ambiguous critical thinking skills that are difficult to define. However, just because the SAT II Subject Tests do a better job of testing your knowledge of a useful subject doesn't mean the tests are necessarily easier or demand less study. A "better" test isn't necessarily better for you in terms of how easy it will be.

In comparison to taking the SAT I, there are good things and bad things about taking an SAT II Subject Test.

The Good

- Because SAT II Subject Tests cover actual topics like grammar, chemistry, and biology, you can study for them effectively. If you don't know a topic in grammar, such as pronoun rules, you can look it up and learn it. The SAT II tests are therefore straightforward tests; if you know your stuff, you will do well on them.

- Often, the classes you've taken in school have already prepared you well for the SAT II. If you've been taking English courses for years, you've probably covered most of the topics that are tested on the SAT II Writing test.

The Bad

- Because SAT II Subject Tests quiz you on specific knowledge, it is much harder to "beat" or "outsmart" an SAT II test than it is to outsmart the SAT I. For the SAT I, you can use all sorts of tricks and strategies to figure out an answer. There are far fewer strategies to help you on the SAT II. Don't get us wrong: having test-taking skills *will* help you on an SAT II, but knowing the subject will help you much, much more. In other words, to do well on the SAT II, you can't just rely on your quick thinking and intelligence. You need to study.

Scoring the SAT II Subject Tests

There are three different versions of your SAT II Writing score. The "raw score" is a simple score of how you did on the test, like the grade you might receive on a normal test in school. The "percentile score" takes your raw score and compares it to the rest of the raw scores in the country, letting you know how you did on the test in comparison to your peers. The "scaled score," which ranges from 200–800, compares your score to the scores received by all students who have ever taken the SAT II.

The Raw Score

You will never know your raw score on the SAT II that you take, because the raw score is not included in the score report. But you should understand how the raw score is calculated, because this knowledge can affect your strategy for approaching the test.

Because the SAT II Writing contains an essay portion in addition to multiple-choice questions, the way its raw score is calculated differs in comparison to most SAT II tests. Calculating your SAT II Writing raw score involves a step beyond what you have to do for the other SAT II tests. Since this chapter of the book is an introduction to all SAT II tests, we're going to describe the usual way that raw scores are calculated. We'll discuss the specifics of how to calculate the SAT II Writing raw score in the next chapter, which begins our specific discussion of the SAT II Writing.

For most SAT II tests, a student's raw score is based solely on the number of questions that student got right, got wrong, and left blank. A correct answer is worth one point; leaving a question blank yields no points; a wrong answer means you lose $1/4$ of a point.

Calculating the raw score is easy. Add up the number of questions you answered correctly and the number of questions answered incorrectly. Then multiply the number of wrong answers by $\frac{1}{4}$, and subtract this value from the number of right answers.

$$\text{raw score} = \text{\# of correct answers} - \frac{1}{4} \times \text{\# of wrong answers}$$

The Percentile Score

Along with the scaled score you receive from the ETS, you will get a percentile score. A student's percentile is based on the percentage of the total test-takers who received a lower raw score than he or she did. Let's say, for example, you had a friend named Zebulon, and he received a score that placed him in the 37th percentile. That 37th percentile tells him that he scored better on the SAT II than 36% of the other students who took the same test; it also means that 63% of the students taking that test scored as well as or better than he did.

The Scaled Score

The scaled score takes the raw score and uses a formula to turn that score into the scaled score from 200–800 that you've probably heard so much about.

The curve to convert raw scores to scaled scores differs from SAT II test to SAT II test. For example, a raw score of 33 on the Math IC will scale to a 600, while the same raw score of 33 on the Math IIC will scale to a 700. In fact, the scaled score can even vary between different editions of the *same* test. A raw score of 33 on the February 2003 Writing might scale to a 710 while a 33 in June 2003 might scale to a 690. These differences in scaled scores exist to accommodate differences in difficulty level and student performance from year to year.

Coleges and the SAT II Subject Tests

We're guessing you didn't sign up to take the SAT II just for the sheer pleasure of it. That's right, you probably want to get into college, and know that the one and only reason to take this test is because colleges want or require you to do so.

Colleges care about SAT II Subject Tests for two related reasons. First, the tests demonstrate your interest, knowledge, and skill in specific topics. Second, because SAT II tests are standardized, they show how your writing (or biology or math) skills measure up to the skills of high school students nationwide. The grades you get in high school don't offer such a measurement to colleges: some high schools are more difficult than others, which means that students of equal ability might receive different grades from different schools, even in English classes that have basically the same curriculum. In contrast, since SAT II tests are national tests, they provide colleges with a definite yardstick against which they can measure your, and every other applicant's, knowledge and skills.

None of this means that SAT II tests are the primary tools that colleges use to decide whether to admit an applicant. High school grades, extracurricular activities, and SAT or ACT scores are all more important to colleges than your scores on SAT II tests. But because SAT II tests provide colleges with such a nice and easy measurement tool, they can add that extra bit of shading that can push your application from the maybe pile into the accepted pile.

When it comes down to it, colleges like the SAT IIs because the tests make the colleges' job easier. The tests are the colleges' tool. But because you know how colleges use the SAT II, you can also look at the tests as your tool. SAT II tests allow colleges to easily compare you to other applicants. This means that the SAT II tests provide you with an excellent chance to shine. If you got a 93% on your English final, and some other kid in some high school across the country got a 91%, colleges don't know how to compare the two grades. They don't know whose class was harder or whose teacher was a tough grader or whose high school inflates grades. But if you get a 720 on the SAT II Writing, and that other kid gets a 650, colleges *will* recognize the difference in your scores. Since the tests can help your application so much, and since preparing for the tests can dramatically improve your score, put some real time and effort into studying for the SAT II tests.

College Placement

Occasionally, colleges use SAT II tests to determine placement. For example, if you do very well on the SAT II Writing, you might be exempted from a basic expository writing class. It's worth finding out whether the colleges to which you are applying use the SAT II tests for placement.

Which SAT II Subject Tests to Take

There are three types of SAT II tests: those you *must* take, those you *should* take, and those you *shouldn't* take.

- The SAT II tests you *must* take are those required by the colleges you are interested in.

- The SAT II tests you *should* take are tests that aren't required, but which you'll do well on, thereby impressing the colleges looking at your application.

• The SAT II tests you *shouldn't* take are those that aren't required and which cover subjects you don't feel confident about.

Determining Which SAT II Tests Are Required

To find out if the colleges to which you are applying require that you take a particular SAT II test, you'll need to do a bit of research. Call the schools you're interested in, look at their web pages online, or talk to your guidance counselor. Often, colleges request that you take the following SAT II tests:

• The SAT II Writing test

• One of the two Math SAT II tests (either Math IC or Math IIC)

• Another SAT II in some other subject of your choice

Not all colleges follow these guidelines, however, so you should take the time to research which tests you need to take in order to apply to the colleges that interest you.

Determining Whether You Should Take an SAT II
Even If It Isn't Required

To decide whether you should take a test that isn't required you have to know two things:

1. What is a good score on that SAT II test

2. Whether you can get that score or higher

Below, we have included a list of the most commonly taken SAT II tests and the average scaled score on each. If you feel confident that you can get a score that is significantly above the average (50 points is significant) taking the test will probably strengthen your college application. Please note that if you are planning to attend an elite school, you might have to score significantly more than 50 points higher than the national average. The following table is just a general guideline. It's a good idea to call the schools that interest you, or talk to a guidance counselor, to get a more precise idea of what score you should be shooting for.

TEST	AVERAGE SCORE
Writing	590–600
Literature	590–600
American History	580–590
World History	570–580
Math IC	580–590
Math IIC	655–665
Biology E/M	590–600
Chemistry	605–615
Physics	635–645

As you decide which test to take, be realistic. Don't just assume you're going to do great without at least taking a practice test and seeing where you stand.

It's a good idea to take three tests that cover a range of subjects, such as one math SAT II, one humanities SAT II (History or Writing), and one science SAT II. However, taking *more* than three SAT II tests is probably not necessary.

When to Take an SAT II Subject Test

The best time to take the SAT II Writing is after you've had as much time as possible in English or writing classes. This does not hold true on all of the SAT II tests—for example, it makes sense to take the Biology test right after finishing a year-long biology course, while the material is fresh in your mind. But the Writing test is not about cramming your head full of formulas and tables; the more total time you've devoted to reading and writing, the better off you'll be. This means that you should take the SAT II Writing sometime during the end of your junior year or the beginning of your senior year.

Unless the colleges to which you are applying use the SAT II for placement purposes, there is no point in taking any SAT II tests after November of your senior year, since you won't get your scores back from ETS until after the application deadline has passed.

ETS usually sets testing dates for SAT II Subject Tests in October, November, December, January, May, and June. However, not every Subject Test is administered in each of these months. To check when the test you want to take is being offered, visit the College Board website at www.collegeboard.com, or do some research in your school's guidance office.

Registering for SAT II Tests

To register for the SAT II test(s) of your choice, you have to fill out some forms and pay a registration fee. We know, we know—it's ridiculous that *you* have to pay for a test that colleges require you to take in order to make *their* jobs easier, but, sadly, there isn't anything we, or you, can do about it. It is acceptable, at this point, to grumble about the unfairness of the world.

After grumbling, however, you still have to register. There are two ways to go about it: online or by mail. To register online, go to www.collegeboard.com and follow the instructions listed. To register by mail, fill out and send in the forms enclosed in the *Registration Bulletin*, which should be available in your high school's guidance office. You can also request a copy of the *Bulletin* by calling the College Board at (609) 771-7600, or writing to:

College Board SAT Program
P.O. Box 6200
Princeton, NJ 08541-6200

You can register to take up to three SAT II tests for any given testing day. Unfortunately, even if you decide to take three tests in one day, you'll have to pay a separate registration fee for each test you take.

Introduction to the SAT II Writing

IMAGINE TWO CHILDREN, Eloise and Bartholomew, racing in the forest. Who will win—Eloise, who never stumbles because she knows the placement of every tree and all the twists and turns and hiding spots, or Bartholomew, who keeps falling down and tripping over roots because he doesn't pay any attention to the landscape? The answer is obvious. Even if Bartholomew is a little faster and more athletic, Eloise will win, because she knows how to navigate the landscape and turn it to her advantage.

This example of a race in the forest illustrates a point: in the metaphor, the structure of the SAT II is the forest, and taking the test is the competition. In this chapter we're going to describe the "landscape" of the SAT II Writing: what topics the questions cover, what the questions look like, and how the questions are organized. In the next chapter, we'll show you the strategies that will allow you to navigate and use the landscape to get the best score you can.

Content of the SAT II Writing

What does ETS test on the SAT II Writing? Not much. The essay portion of the SAT II tests your general writing skills; the multiple-choice portion tests your knowledge of the following grammar and writing rules:

- Verb tense agreement

- Pronoun rules

11

- Parallelism
- Noun agreement
- Subject-verb agreement
- Coordination and subordination
- Logical comparison
- Misplaced modifiers
- Diction
- Wordiness
- Idiom
- Sentence fragments and run-ons
- Double negatives

The SAT II Writing test does *not* cover:

- Spelling
- Punctuation
- Technical names of grammar and writing rules

Because of the limited material tested, and because you will never have to know grammar terms, you should not feel daunted or panicked as you set out to study for this test. In essence, the Writing test doesn't test your ability to understand grammar so much as it tests your ability to "hear" wrong grammar. You see, in order to do well on this test, you need to be able to identify only two things: sentences that sound strange, and sentences that sound right. On one section of the test, you'll have to know how to fix up a strange sentence so it sounds right. On the essay section, you'll have to know how to generate your own right sentences. If you can sniff out a bad sentence, you're well on your way to doing well on the SAT II Writing.

How Reading Trashy Magazines Will Help Your Score

The most important tool to cultivate before test day is your reading ear: you want to be able to "hear" errors as you read the test sentences. One excellent way to nurture your reading ear is to actually read. Regardless of whether you start preparing a year, a month, or a week before you plan to take the SAT II Writing, you should start reading for an hour every day. Reading instant messages, or reading the book you're assigned for English class as you simultaneously watch television—this kind of reading does not count. Read novels, or the newspaper; if you've had a terrible day and can't face the next chapter or the metro section, read a trashy magazine, but read it carefully and without distractions.

When you read something well-written, you see correct sentence structure and grammar over and over and over. Soon, correctly written sentences become familiar to you. After you read several thousand good sentences, a bad sentence will seem painfully obvious. That's the goal of all this reading: when you sit down to the SAT II Writing, you want to look at those sentences and see each error as quickly and clearly as if it were highlighted, italicized, and printed in bold.

Reading will also help you enormously on the essay. As you're writing the essay, if you have that good-sentence groove carved into your brain, all you have to do is model your sentence structure on all of the thousands of grammatically correct sentences you've read in your novels and magazines, and you'll be writing well.

Format of the SAT II Writing

The SAT II Writing test is a one-hour-long test composed of one essay and 60 multiple-choice questions. The multiple-choice questions come in three types: 30 Identifying Sentence Error questions, 18 Improving Sentences questions, and 12 Improving Paragraphs questions. On the test, you'll encounter the different sections in the following order:

- The Essay

- 20 Identifying Sentence Error questions

- 18 Improving Sentences questions

- 12 Improving Paragraphs questions

- 10 Identifying Sentence Error questions

The Essay Section

You will have 20 minutes to plan and write one essay. After the 20 minutes are up, you will be forced to stop writing the essay, even if you're not done. If you finish writing the essay early, which is pretty unlikely, you can proceed right to the multiple-choice section of the test.

The Multiple-Choice Questions

You will have 40 minutes to answer the 60 multiple-choice questions. Below, you'll find a very brief overview of each type of question, including a sample question.

Identifying Sentence Errors

As the name implies, your sole task on this type of multiple-choice question involves finding errors. That's all you have to do. You don't have to fix the errors, name them, or do anything other than spot them. Commonly tested subjects on this section are subject-verb agreement and verb tense.

Questions will look like this:

> Even though the influx of people <u>has raised</u> rents citywide, <u>there is</u> many financial
>   A   B
>
> gains <u>to be had</u> from the new <u>residents</u>. <u>No error</u>
>   C   D   E

In this example, the correct answer is (B); the phrase *there is* uses a singular verb when it should use the plural verb *are* to match the plural subject *gains*. The original sentence has faulty subject-verb agreement.

Improving Sentences

Each question in the Improving Sentences section consists of a sentence with one portion underlined. You must decide if the underlined portion contains an error. If it does not, mark (A), no error. If it does, find the answer choice that corrects the problem.

Questions will look like this:

> In her excitement about her trip to Paris, Emily has studied French with great <u>enthusiasm, thus she completely neglects her Spanish class</u>.
>
> (A)   enthusiasm, thus she completely neglects her Spanish class
> (B)   enthusiasm she completely neglects her Spanish class as a result
> (C)   enthusiasm and thus has completely neglected her Spanish class
> (D)   enthusiasm; her Spanish class neglected therefore
> (E)   enthusiasm; her Spanish class is neglected by this

The correct answer is (C). The original sentence is a run-on sentence, which (C) corrects by adding *and* as a conjunction.

Improving Paragraphs

For this type of question, you'll be given two short essays that are purportedly written by students. You'll read the essay and then answer six to eight questions about it. These questions fall under four categories:

1. sentence revision questions

2. sentence addition questions

3. sentence combination questions

4. analysis questions

These questions will look something like this:

Sentence Revision

> Which of the answer choices below is the best way of revising the underlined part of sentence 7 (reprinted below)?

Sentence Addition

> Which of the sentences below, if added after sentence 10, would provide the best transition from the first paragraph to the second paragraph?

Sentence Combination

> Which of the following is the best way to combine sentences 3 and 4 (reprinted below)?

Analysis

> All of the following are techniques the writer uses EXCEPT:

Most Improving Paragraphs questions fall into the category of sentence revision, but most tests contain at least one question of each type.

Rules of the Test

In addition to the content and format of the test, there are some rules of the SAT II Writing that the directions will not tell you, but that are very important to know.

- When taking the test, you can skip around between sections. You must write the essay first, but after that, you can do the sections in any order you like. For example, if you find that the Identifying Sentence Error questions are easy for you, you can answer those thirty questions before turning to the Improving Sentences and Improving Paragraphs questions.

- The questions on the test aren't organized by difficulty. In other words, a difficult question about word choice might be followed by an easy question about subject-verb agreement.

- All questions are worth the same number of points. You will not get more points for answering a difficult question, or fewer points for answering an easy question.

These three rules greatly affect how you should approach the test. We will explain how and why in the next chapter, which discusses general strategy for the SAT II Writing.

Scoring the SAT II Writing Test

As we said previously, because the SAT II Writing test contains an essay as well as multiple-choice questions, calculating your raw score for this test is a little more complicated than it is for other SAT II tests.

To calculate your total raw score for the SAT II Writing, you need to calculate your raw scores for the essay and for the multiple-choice, and then add the two together. Calculating your raw score for the multiple-choice is easy. Just follow the normal procedures:

$$\text{multiple-choice raw score } = \text{ \# of correct answers} - \frac{\text{\# of wrong answers}}{4}$$

Calculating your essay raw score is also easy. Take the grade that you receive on your essay, which can range between 2–12, and multiply that number by 3.43.

$$\text{essay raw score } = \text{ essay score} \times 3.43$$

The number 3.43 seems like a strange and arbitrary number, but the test writers use this multiplication by the number 3.43 to make the essay have the precise weight in your final score that they want.

Your total raw score is the sum of your multiple-choice raw score and essay raw score:

$$\text{Total Raw Score } = \text{ multiple-choice raw score} + \text{essay raw score}$$

ETS takes this raw score and converts it to a scaled score according to a special curve. We have included a generalized version of that curve in a table below. (Note that because ETS changes the curve slightly for each edition of the test, this table will be close to, but not exactly the same as, the table used by ETS.)

Raw Score	Scaled Score	Raw Score	Scaled Score	Raw Score	Scaled Score
101	800	63	560	25	370
100	800	62	560	24	370
99	800	61	550	23	360
98	800	60	550	22	360
97	800	59	540	21	350
96	800	58	540	20	350
95	800	57	530	19	340
94	800	56	530	18	340

Raw Score	Scaled Score	Raw Score	Scaled Score	Raw Score	Scaled Score
93	800	55	520	17	330
92	790	54	520	16	330
91	780	53	510	15	320
90	770	52	510	14	320
89	760	51	500	13	310
88	750	50	500	12	310
87	740	49	490	11	300
86	740	48	490	10	300
85	730	47	480	9	300
84	720	46	480	8	290
83	710	45	470	7	290
82	700	44	470	6	280
81	690	43	460	5	280
80	680	42	460	4	280
79	680	41	450	3	270
78	670	40	450	2	270
77	660	39	440	1	260
76	650	38	440	0	260
75	650	37	430	−1	260
74	640	36	430	−2	260
73	630	35	420	−3	250
72	620	34	420	−4	250
71	610	33	410	−5	250
70	600	32	410	−6	250
69	600	31	400	−7	240
68	600	30	400	−8	240
67	590	29	390	−9	240
66	590	28	390	−10	230
65	580	27	380		
64	570	26	380		

You should use this chart to convert your raw score into a scaled score. In order to do so, you will have to grade your essay in some way. Perhaps a parent or teacher can help you, if you explain the criteria by which an essay is graded.

The Writing SAT II

If you can't find anyone to grade your essay, you can use the conversion chart below to get a sense of how you're doing in the mutiple-choice section.

Raw Score	Scaled Score	Raw Score	Scaled Score	Raw Score	Scaled Score
60	80	36	55	12	40
59	80	35	55	11	39
58	79	34	54	10	38
57	78	33	54	9	37
56	77	32	52	8	37
55	75	31	52	7	36
54	74	30	51	6	35
53	72	29	51	5	35
52	71	28	50	4	34
51	70	27	50	3	33
50	69	26	49	2	32
49	67	25	48	1	31
48	66	24	48	0	30
47	65	23	47	−1	30
46	65	22	46	−2	29
45	64	21	46	−3	28
44	63	20	45	−4	27
43	62	19	44	−5	26
42	61	18	43	−6	25
41	60	17	43	−7	24
40	59	16	42	−8	23
39	58	15	42	−9	23
38	57	14	41	−10	22
37	56	13	40		

In addition to their function as conversion tables, these charts contain crucial information: they tell you that you can do very well on the Writing SAT II without writing a perfect essay or answering every question correctly. In fact, you could skip some questions and get some other questions wrong and still earn a perfect score of 800.

For example, in a test of 60 questions, you could score:

Score	Multiple-choice right	Multiple-choice wrong	Blank	Essay score
800	55	2	3	12
800	58	2	0	11
750	55	4	1	10
700	52	5	3	10
650	48	6	6	10
600	42	8	10	10
550	36	9	15	8

This chart should prove to you that when you're taking the test, you should not imagine your score plummeting with every question you can't confidently answer. You can do very well on this test without knowing or answering everything. The key is to follow a strategy that ensures that you will get to see and answer all the questions you can answer correctly, and then to guess intelligently on those questions about which you are a little unsure. We will discuss these strategies in the next chapter.

Strategies for the SAT II Writing

A MACHINE, NOT A PERSON, will score the multiple-choice questions on the SAT II Writing test. The tabulating machine sees only the filled-in ovals on your answer sheet and does not care how you came to these answers; it just impassively notes whether your answers are correct. So whether you knew the right answer immediately or just took a lucky guess, the machine will award you one point. It doesn't award extra points if you've spent a really long time getting the right answer. It doesn't award extra points if you managed to get a tricky question right. Think of the multiple-choice test as a message to you from the ETS: "We care only about your answers. We do not care about the work behind those answers."

So you should give ETS right answers, as many as possible, using whatever means possible. The SAT II Writing test not only allows you to show off your intelligence and your knowledge of writing, it allows you to show off your fox-like cunning by figuring out what strategies will allow you to best display that knowledge. Remember, the SAT II test is your tool to get into college, so treat it as your tool. It wants right answers? Give it right answers, by using whatever strategies you can.

In this chapter, you'll learn a number of strategies that will help you maximize your score and avoid making errors on the SAT II Writing.

Avoid Carelessness

Avoiding carelessness probably sounds to you more like common sense than like a sophisticated strategy. We don't disagree. But it is amazing how a timed test can warp and mangle common sense.

There are two types of carelessness, both of which will cost you points. The first type of carelessness results from moving too fast, whether that speed is caused by overconfidence or fear. In speeding through the test, you make yourself vulnerable to misinterpreting the question, overlooking one of the answer choices, or simply making a careless mistake. As you take the test, make a conscious effort to approach the test calmly.

Whereas the first type of carelessness can be caused by overconfidence, the second type of carelessness results from frustration or lack of confidence. Some students take a defeatist attitude toward tests, assuming they won't be able to answer many of the questions. Such an attitude is a form of carelessness, because it causes the student to ignore reality. Just as the overconfident student assumes she can't be tricked and therefore gets tricked, the student without confidence assumes he can't answer questions and therefore gives up at the first sign of difficulty.

Both kinds of carelessness steal points from you. Avoid them.

Be Careful Gridding In Your Answers

The computer that scores SAT II tests is unmerciful. If you answered a question correctly, but somehow made a mistake in marking your answer grid, the computer will mark that question as wrong. If you skipped question 5, but put the answer to question 6 in row 5 and the answer to question 7 in row 6, etc., thereby throwing off your answers for an entire section . . . it gets ugly.

Some test-prep books advise that you fill in your answer sheet five questions at a time rather than one at a time. Some suggest that you do one question and then fill in the corresponding bubble. We think you should fill out the answer sheet whatever way feels most natural to you. Just make sure you're careful while doing it. In our opinion, the best way to ensure that you're being careful is to talk silently to yourself. As you figure out an answer in the test booklet and transfer it over to the answer sheet ovals, say to yourself: "Number 23, B. Number 24, E. Number 25, A."

Guessing and the SAT II Writing

Should you guess on the SAT II Writing? We'll begin to answer this question by posing a math question:

> Shakespeare is holding five cards, numbered 1–5. Without telling you, he has selected one
> of the numbered cards as the "correct" one. If you pick a single card, what is the probability
> that you will choose the "correct" card?

The answer is $1/5$, or 1 in 5. But the answer is only important if you recognize that the question precisely describes the situation you're in when you blindly guess the answer to any SAT II Writing question. When guessing blindly, you have a $1/5$ chance of getting the question right. If you were to guess on ten questions, you would, according to probability, get two questions right and eight questions wrong.

- 2 right answers gets you 2 raw points

- 8 wrong answers gets you $8 \times -1/4 = -2$ raw points

Those ten answers, therefore, net you a total of *0* points. Blind guessing is a complete waste of time, which is precisely what ETS wants. They designed the scoring system to make blind guessing pointless.

Educated Guessing

But what if your guessing isn't blind? Suppose you're faced with this question:

> The yodelers <u>drew</u> lots of people, for <u>it</u> had never <u>appeared</u> on stage <u>before</u>. <u>No error</u>

Suppose that this question flummoxes you. The directions tell you to find the error in the sentence and pick the corresponding answer choice, but you can't seem to find the error. You stare at the question and realize that the only underlined word you confidently feel is correct is *before*. The other ones look like they might be wrong. Since you're almost certain *before* is correct, you eliminate (D). Once you've eliminated *before* as a possible answer, you have four choices from which to choose. Is it now worth it to guess? *Yes.* Probability states that if you are guessing between four choices you will get one question right for every three you get wrong. For that one correct answer you'll get 1 point, and for the three incorrect answers you'll lose a total of $3/4$ of a point.

$$1 - \frac{3}{4} = \frac{1}{4}$$

In other words, if you can eliminate one answer, the odds of guessing turn in your favor. You become more likely to gain points than to lose points.

The rule for guessing on the SAT II Writing, therefore, is simple: *if you can eliminate even one answer choice on a question, you should definitely guess.*

If You're Stumped

If you cannot eliminate even one answer choice and find yourself staring at a certain question with mounting panic, throw a circle around that nasty question and move on. If you have time later, you can return to that question. Remember, answering a hard question correctly doesn't earn you any more points than answering an easy question correctly. You want to be sure to hit every easy question instead of running out of time by fixating on the really tough questions. While taking five minutes to solve a particularly difficult question might strike you as a moral victory when you're taking the test, quite possibly you could have used that same time to answer six other questions that would have vastly increased your score. Instead of getting bogged down on individual questions, you will do better if you learn to skip, and leave for later, the very difficult questions that you can't answer or that will take an extremely long time to answer.

Pacing

Good pacing allows you to take the test, rather than letting the test take you. As we said earlier, the questions on the SAT II Writing test are not organized by difficulty. You are as likely to come upon a question you can answer at the end of the test as at the beginning. As you take the test, part of your job is to make sure that you don't miss out on answering those questions near the end of the test that you could have answered if only you had more time.

By perfecting your pacing on practice tests, you can make sure that you will see every question on the test. And if you see every question on the test, then you can select which questions you will and won't answer, rather than running out of time before reaching the end of the test and therefore letting the test decide, by default, which questions you won't answer.

In large part, pacing yourself entails putting into practice the strategies we've already discussed:

- Make sure not to get bogged down on one single question. If you find yourself wasting time on one question, circle it, move on, and come back to it later.

- Answer every question for which you know the answer, and make an educated guess for every question for which you can quickly eliminate at least one answer choice.

Learning to pace yourself is a crucial part of your preparation for the test. Students who know how to pace themselves take the test on their own terms. Students who don't know how to pace themselves enter the test already one step behind.

Setting a Target Score

You can make the job of pacing yourself much easier if you go into the test knowing how many questions you have to answer correctly in order to earn the score you want. So, what score do you want? Obviously, you should strive for the best score possible, but also be realistic: consider how much you know about writing and how well you do, generally, on SAT-type tests. You should also consider what exactly defines a good score at the colleges to which you're applying: a 620? A 680? Talk to the admissions offices of the colleges you might want to attend, do a little research in college guidebooks, or talk to your guidance counselor. No matter how you do it, you should find out the average score of students at the schools you want to attend. Take that number and set your target score above it (you want to be above average, right?). Then take a look at this chart we showed you before.

Score	Multiple-choice right	Multiple-choice wrong	Blank	Essay score
800	55	2	3	12
800	58	2	0	11
750	55	4	1	10
700	52	5	3	10
650	48	6	6	10
600	42	8	10	10
550	36	9	15	8

So let's say the average score for the SAT II Writing for the school you want to attend is a 600. You should set your target at about 650. Looking at this chart, you can see that, to get that score, you need to get 48 questions right. You can get 6 questions wrong and leave 6 questions blank. You also need to get a 10 on the essay.

If you know all these numbers going into the test, you can pace yourself accordingly. You should use practice tests to teach yourself the proper pace—increasing your speed if you find that you aren't getting to answer all the questions you need to, or decreasing your pace if you find that you're rushing and making careless mistakes. If you reach your target score during preparation, give yourself a cookie and take a break for the day. But just because you hit your target score doesn't mean you should stop working altogether. In fact, you should view reaching your target score as a clue that you can do *better* than that score: set a new target 50–100 points above your original and work to pick up your pace a little bit and skip fewer questions.

By improving in manageable increments, you can slowly work up to your top speed, integrating your new knowledge of the test and how to take it without overwhelming yourself by trying to take on too much too soon. If you can handle working just a little faster without becoming careless and losing points, your score will certainly go up. If you meet your new target score again, repeat the process.

Practice Tests

Practice Tests Are Your Best Friends

BELIEVE IT OR NOT, THE SAT II WRITING test has some redeeming qualities. One of them: reliability. The dear old thing doesn't change much from year to year. You can always count on a bunch of questions about subject-verb agreement and tense in the Identifying Sentence Errors section. You'll always see run-on sentences, passive voice, and parallelism errors tested in the Improving Sentences section. Revision questions will abound in the Improving Paragraphs section, and come hell or high water, you'll always have to write an essay in response to a statement.

Obviously, different editions of the SAT II Writing aren't *exactly* the same; individual questions will never repeat from test to test. But the subjects that those questions test, and the way in which the questions test those subjects, *will* stay constant.

This constancy can be of great benefit to you as you study for the test. To show how you can use the similarity between different versions of the SAT II Writing test to your own advantage, we provide a case study.

Using the Similarity of the SAT II Writing for Personal Gain

Suppose you sit down in a quiet room and spend an hour taking the practice test. Once you've completed the test, you flip to the back of the book and check your answers. You get to question 10 and notice that you got it wrong. You look back at the question, and see that number 10 asked about this sentence:

> At a crucial juncture in the movie, someone reached for their box of candy and loudly removed the plastic packaging.

You chose (E), no error, which turns out to be the wrong answer. As you puzzle over the question, you realize that you don't understand why you got the answer wrong. The sentence looks perfectly fine to you! You turn to the explanations and learn that the error is the pronoun *their*, which people often use incorrectly in speech in an effort to avoid using a gender-specific singular pronoun. You realize that you didn't catch the error in number 10 (which should read, by the way, *At a crucial juncture in the movie, someone reached for his or her box of candy and loudly removed the plastic packaging*) because you didn't understand that *their* is incorrect in that context: *someone* is singular and must be matched with a singular pronoun. You now promise that you will exercise extra caution when you see *their* in a sentence. Also, you now feel confident and smart, because you understand one of the rules governing pronouns.

Analyzing Your Post-Practice Test Performance

Sometimes you'll answer a question wrong not because you weren't paying attention, and not because you were rushing, but because, as in the example above, you truly didn't understand the material being tested. When you are checking over your practice test, it's crucial to figure out *why* you got wrong what you got wrong. It's a bad idea to simply see that you got an answer wrong and continue on your merry way. It's a good idea to do what the hypothetical you did when faced with question number 10: go back to the question and figure out why you got it wrong and what you need to know to get it right.

Skeptical readers might say, "Sure, but I'll never see that question again. I'll never have to examine that sentence about the rude moviegoer on the real SAT II Writing, so isn't figuring out my mistake a waste of time?"

No! It's definitely *not* a waste of time. The reason: if you take the time to learn why you got a question wrong, and to learn the material you need to know to get it right, you'll probably remember what you've learned the next time you're faced with a similar question. And chances are excellent that you will be faced with a similar question.

Sure, you won't see exactly the same sentences you saw on the practice test, but you'll see sentences that test exactly the same rules. Learn the rules when you're checking your practice tests, and you'll remember the rules when you're taking the real thing.

But What if I Get a Lot of Questions Wrong on the Practice Test?

What if you take a practice test and get a whole bunch of questions wrong, and it turns out you're shaky not just on pronoun rules, but on parallelism and run-on sentences and tense errors and misplaced modifiers? Instead of throwing up your hands in despair and flopping down on the couch to watch TV, make yourself identify all of the questions you got wrong, figure out why you got them wrong, and then teach yourself what you should have done to get these questions right. If you can't figure out your error, find someone who can. *Study* your completed practice test.

Think about it. What does an incorrect answer mean? That wrong answer identifies a weakness in your test taking, whether that weakness is an unfamiliarity with a particular topic or a tendency to be careless. If you got fifteen questions wrong on a practice test, then each of those fifteen questions identifies a weakness in your knowledge about the topics the SAT II Writing tests. But as you study each question and figure out why you got that question wrong, you are actually learning how to answer the very questions that will appear, in similar form, on the real SAT II Writing. You are discovering your SAT II Writing weaknesses and addressing them, and you are learning to understand not just the knowledge behind the question, but the way that ETS asks its questions as well.

True, if you got fifteen questions wrong, the first time you study your test will take quite a bit of time. But if you invest that time and study your practice test properly, you will be eliminating future mistakes. Each successive practice test you take should have fewer errors, meaning you'll need to spend less time studying those errors. Also, and more importantly, you'll be pinpointing what you need to study for the real SAT II Writing, identifying and overcoming your weaknesses, and learning to answer an increasing variety of questions on the specific topics covered by the test. Taking practice tests and studying them will allow you to teach yourself how to recognize and handle whatever the SAT II Writing has to throw at you.

Taking a Practice Test

Now you know a bit about what to do when you're finished taking the test. Let's backtrack and talk about what to do while you're actually taking the practice test.

Controlling Your Environment

Although a practice test is practice, and no one but you needs to see your scores, you should do everything in your power to make the practice test feel like the real SAT II Writing. The closer your practice resembles the real thing, the more helpful it will be.

When taking a practice test, follow these rules:

Take the tests timed. Don't give yourself any extra time. Be stricter with yourself than the meanest proctor you can think of would be. Also, don't give yourself time off for bathroom breaks. If you have to go to the bathroom, let the clock keep running; that's what'll happen on the real SAT II.

Take the test in a single sitting. Training yourself to endure an hour of test taking is part of your preparation.

Find a place to take the test that holds no distractions. Don't take the practice test in a room with lots of people walking through it. Go to a library, your bedroom, a well-lit closet, anywhere quiet. Otherwise your concentration won't be what it should be and your practice test won't reflect your true capabilities, or your true weaknesses.

These are the rules of taking practice tests. Now, having stated them, we can relax a little bit: don't be so strict with yourself that studying and taking practice tests becomes unbearable. The most important thing is that you actually study. Do whatever you have to do in order to make your studying interesting and painless enough that you actually do it.

Ultimately, if you can follow all of the above rules to the letter, you will probably be better off. But, if following those rules makes studying excruciating, find little ways to bend them that won't interfere too much with your concentration.

Practice Test Strategy

You should take each practice test as if it were the real SAT II Writing. Don't be more daring than you would be on the actual test, guessing blindly even when you can't eliminate an answer; don't carelessly speed through the test. Don't flip through this book while taking the practice exam just to sneak a peek. Follow the rules for guessing and for skipping questions that we outlined in the chapter on strategy. The more closely your attitude and strategies during the practice test reflect those you'll employ during the actual test, the more predictive the practice test will be of your strengths and weaknesses and the more fruitful your studying of the test will be.

Scoring Your Practice Test

After you take your practice test, you'll no doubt want to score it and see how you did. When you do your scoring, don't just write down how many questions you answered correctly and incorrectly and tally up your score. Instead, keep a list of every question you got wrong and every question you skipped. This list will be your guide when you study your test.

Studying Your . . . No, Wait, Go Take a Break

Go relax for a while. You know how to do that.

Studying Your Practice Test

After grading your test, you should have a list of the questions you answered incorrectly or skipped. Studying your test involves going through this list and examining each question you answered incorrectly. When you look at each question, you shouldn't just look to see what the correct answer is, but rather why you got the question wrong and how you could have gotten the question right. Train yourself in the process of getting the question right.

Why did you get the question wrong?

There are three main reasons why you might have gotten an individual question wrong.

Reason 1: You thought you knew the answer, but actually you didn't.

Reason 2: You managed to eliminate some answer choices and then guessed among the remaining answers; sadly, you guessed wrong.

Reason 3: You knew the answer but made a careless mistake.
You should know which of these reasons applies to every question you got wrong.

What could you have done to get the question right?

The reasons you got a question wrong affect how you should think about it while studying your test.

If You Got a Question Wrong for Reason 1, Lack of Knowledge:

A question answered in-correctly for Reason 1 identifies a weakness in your knowledge of the material tested on the SAT II Writing. Discovering this wrong answer gives you an opportunity to target your weakness. When addressing that weakness, make sure that you don't look solely at that question; study the rule governing that question, too. Say you get an Improving Paragraphs question wrong that asks you to combine two sentences. Don't just note that the right answer involved combining the sentences using a comma and a conjunction; study the other ways you can combine sentences, and look at the ways people commonly combine sentences incorrectly. Remember, you will *not* see a question exactly like the question you got wrong. But you probably *will* see a question that covers the same topic as the practice question. For that reason, when you get a question wrong, don't just figure out the right answer to the question—learn the broader topic of which the question tests only a piece.

If You Got a Question Wrong for Reason 2, Guessing Wrong:

If you guessed wrong, review your guessing strategy. Did you guess smartly? Could you have eliminated more answers? If yes, why didn't you? By thinking in this critical way about the decisions you made while taking the practice test, you can train yourself to make quicker, more decisive, and better decisions.

If you took a guess and chose the incorrect answer, don't let that sour you on guessing. Even as you go over the question and figure out if there was any way for you to have answered the question without having to guess, remind yourself that if you eliminated at least one answer and guessed, even if you got the question wrong, you followed the right strategy.

If You Got a Question Wrong for Reason 3, Carelessness:

If you discover you got a question wrong because you were careless, it might be tempting to say to yourself, "Oh I made a careless error," and assure yourself you won't do that again. That is not enough. You made that careless mistake for a reason, and you should try to figure out why. Whereas getting a question wrong because you didn't know the answer constitutes a weakness in your knowledge about the test, making a careless mistake represents a weakness in your *method of taking the test*. To overcome this weakness, you need to approach it in the same critical way you would approach a lack of knowledge. Study your mistake. Reenact your thought process on the problem and see where and how your carelessness came about: were you rushing? Did you jump at the first answer that seemed right instead of reading all the answers? Know your error and look it in the eye. If you learn precisely what your mistake was, you are much less likely to make that mistake again.

If You Left the Question Blank

It is also a good idea to study the questions you left blank on the test, since those questions constitute a reservoir of lost points. If you left the question blank, then a different thinking applies. A blank answer is a result either of:

1. Total inability to answer a question

2. Lack of time

In the case of the first possibility, you should see if there was some way you might have been able to eliminate an answer choice or two and put yourself in a better position to guess. In the second case, look over the question and see whether you think you could have answered it. If you definitely could have, then you know that you are throwing away points and probably working too slowly. If you couldn't, then carry out the above steps: study the relevant material and review your guessing strategy.

The Secret Weapon: Talking to Yourself

Yeah, it's embarrassing. Yeah, you might look silly. But talking to yourself is perhaps the best way to pound something into your brain. As you go through the steps of studying a question, you should talk them out. When you verbalize something, it makes it much harder to delude yourself into thinking that you're working if you're really not.

We are serious about this advice. Of course, it is just a suggestion. We can't enforce it and, anyway, we don't want to. But it is a nice little study trick. And it will help you.

SAT II Writing Test 1

WRITING TEST 1 ANSWER SHEET

1. Ⓐ Ⓑ Ⓒ Ⓓ Ⓔ	21. Ⓐ Ⓑ Ⓒ Ⓓ Ⓔ	41. Ⓐ Ⓑ Ⓒ Ⓓ Ⓔ
2. Ⓐ Ⓑ Ⓒ Ⓓ Ⓔ	22. Ⓐ Ⓑ Ⓒ Ⓓ Ⓔ	42. Ⓐ Ⓑ Ⓒ Ⓓ Ⓔ
3. Ⓐ Ⓑ Ⓒ Ⓓ Ⓔ	23. Ⓐ Ⓑ Ⓒ Ⓓ Ⓔ	43. Ⓐ Ⓑ Ⓒ Ⓓ Ⓔ
4. Ⓐ Ⓑ Ⓒ Ⓓ Ⓔ	24. Ⓐ Ⓑ Ⓒ Ⓓ Ⓔ	44. Ⓐ Ⓑ Ⓒ Ⓓ Ⓔ
5. Ⓐ Ⓑ Ⓒ Ⓓ Ⓔ	25. Ⓐ Ⓑ Ⓒ Ⓓ Ⓔ	45. Ⓐ Ⓑ Ⓒ Ⓓ Ⓔ
6. Ⓐ Ⓑ Ⓒ Ⓓ Ⓔ	26. Ⓐ Ⓑ Ⓒ Ⓓ Ⓔ	46. Ⓐ Ⓑ Ⓒ Ⓓ Ⓔ
7. Ⓐ Ⓑ Ⓒ Ⓓ Ⓔ	27. Ⓐ Ⓑ Ⓒ Ⓓ Ⓔ	47. Ⓐ Ⓑ Ⓒ Ⓓ Ⓔ
8. Ⓐ Ⓑ Ⓒ Ⓓ Ⓔ	28. Ⓐ Ⓑ Ⓒ Ⓓ Ⓔ	48. Ⓐ Ⓑ Ⓒ Ⓓ Ⓔ
9. Ⓐ Ⓑ Ⓒ Ⓓ Ⓔ	29. Ⓐ Ⓑ Ⓒ Ⓓ Ⓔ	49. Ⓐ Ⓑ Ⓒ Ⓓ Ⓔ
10. Ⓐ Ⓑ Ⓒ Ⓓ Ⓔ	30. Ⓐ Ⓑ Ⓒ Ⓓ Ⓔ	50. Ⓐ Ⓑ Ⓒ Ⓓ Ⓔ
11. Ⓐ Ⓑ Ⓒ Ⓓ Ⓔ	31. Ⓐ Ⓑ Ⓒ Ⓓ Ⓔ	51. Ⓐ Ⓑ Ⓒ Ⓓ Ⓔ
12. Ⓐ Ⓑ Ⓒ Ⓓ Ⓔ	32. Ⓐ Ⓑ Ⓒ Ⓓ Ⓔ	52. Ⓐ Ⓑ Ⓒ Ⓓ Ⓔ
13. Ⓐ Ⓑ Ⓒ Ⓓ Ⓔ	33. Ⓐ Ⓑ Ⓒ Ⓓ Ⓔ	53. Ⓐ Ⓑ Ⓒ Ⓓ Ⓔ
14. Ⓐ Ⓑ Ⓒ Ⓓ Ⓔ	34. Ⓐ Ⓑ Ⓒ Ⓓ Ⓔ	54. Ⓐ Ⓑ Ⓒ Ⓓ Ⓔ
15. Ⓐ Ⓑ Ⓒ Ⓓ Ⓔ	35. Ⓐ Ⓑ Ⓒ Ⓓ Ⓔ	55. Ⓐ Ⓑ Ⓒ Ⓓ Ⓔ
16. Ⓐ Ⓑ Ⓒ Ⓓ Ⓔ	36. Ⓐ Ⓑ Ⓒ Ⓓ Ⓔ	56. Ⓐ Ⓑ Ⓒ Ⓓ Ⓔ
17. Ⓐ Ⓑ Ⓒ Ⓓ Ⓔ	37. Ⓐ Ⓑ Ⓒ Ⓓ Ⓔ	57. Ⓐ Ⓑ Ⓒ Ⓓ Ⓔ
18. Ⓐ Ⓑ Ⓒ Ⓓ Ⓔ	38. Ⓐ Ⓑ Ⓒ Ⓓ Ⓔ	58. Ⓐ Ⓑ Ⓒ Ⓓ Ⓔ
19. Ⓐ Ⓑ Ⓒ Ⓓ Ⓔ	39. Ⓐ Ⓑ Ⓒ Ⓓ Ⓔ	59. Ⓐ Ⓑ Ⓒ Ⓓ Ⓔ
20. Ⓐ Ⓑ Ⓒ Ⓓ Ⓔ	40. Ⓐ Ⓑ Ⓒ Ⓓ Ⓔ	60. Ⓐ Ⓑ Ⓒ Ⓓ Ⓔ

WRITING TEST

Part A

Time — 20 minutes

You have twenty minutes to plan and write an essay on the topic assigned below. DO NOT WRITE ON ANOTHER TOPIC. AN ESSAY ON ANOTHER TOPIC IS NOT ACCEPTABLE.

The essay is assigned to give you an opportunity to show how well you can write. You should, therefore, take care to express your thoughts on the topic clearly and effectively. How well you write is much more important than how much you write, but to cover the topic adequately you will probably need to write more than one paragraph. Be specific.

Your essay must be written on the following two pages. You will find that you have enough space if you write on every line, avoid wide margins, and keep your handwriting to a reasonable size. It is important to remember that what you write will be read by someone who is not familiar with your handwriting. Try to write or print so that what you are writing is legible to the reader.

Consider the following statement and assignment. Then write the essay as directed.

"Every event can be viewed from multiple perspectives." *Religion*

Assignment: Choose one example from personal experience, current events, or history, literature, or any other discipline and use this example to write an essay in which you agree or disagree with the statement above. Your essay should be specific.

DO NOT WRITE YOUR ESSAY IN YOUR TEST BOOK. You will receive credit only for what you write on your answer sheet.

WHEN YOUR SUPERVISOR ANNOUNCES THAT TWENTY MINUTES HAVE PASSED, YOU MUST STOP WRITING THE ESSAY AND GO ON TO PART B IF YOU HAVE NOT ALREADY DONE SO. IF YOU FINISH YOUR ESSAY BEFORE THIS ANNOUNCEMENT, GO ON TO PART B AT ONCE.

BEGIN WRITING YOUR ESSAY ON THE ANSWER SHEET.

WRITING TEST

Part A

Time — 20 minutes

The work of religious scriptures are interpreted in various ways. Scholars in this day research and form their theories of events in these scriptures. Lets focus on the 3 main texts: Quran, Torah, and the Bible. because each book are read and interpreted every day.

The saying "Every event can be viewed from multiple prespectives" resonates with the religious scriptures because there are events from history that are written differently in each text. For example, when looking at the story of Jesus, the Quran states that Jesus was not resurrected, but he was a prophet unlike the Bible. in

These are historical texts that contain recorded events, stories, and parables, which can be subject and objective. When looking at all the prespectives, from each scripture evidence, we can connect the dots and be closer to a truth.

Similarly, historical evidence holds its form of subjectivity because the evidence is written from 1 perspective, when looking us

WRITING TEST

Part A

Time — 20 minutes

more primary sources, we can form a clearer conclusion to the objectivity of the time period.

All in all, it is essential for historians, and religious scholars to look at historical sources at a detective manner because there can be more evidence to look at to find a truth and see what really happened. Every human thinks differently but we have to work to understand one another and look at other's way of thinking.

WRITING TEST

Part B

Time — 40 minutes

Directions: The following sentences test your knowledge of grammar, usage, diction (choice of words), and idiom.

Some sentences are correct.
No sentence contains more than one error.

You will find that the error, if there is one, is underlined and lettered. Elements of the sentence that are not underlined will not be changed. In choosing answers, follow the requirements of standard written English.

If there is an error, select the <u>one underlined part</u> that must be changed to make the sentence correct and fill in the corresponding oval on your answer sheet.

If there is no answer, fill in answer oval Ⓔ.

EXAMPLE:

<u>The other</u> delegates and <u>him</u> <u>immediately</u>
   A   B   C

accepted the resolution <u>drafted by</u> the
                    D

neutral states. <u>No error</u>
            E

SAMPLE ANSWER:

Ⓐ ● Ⓒ Ⓓ Ⓔ

---

1. Kristine was soon <u>to</u> learn that she could make <u>herself</u>
              A   B

understood more <u>easily</u> by speaking French <u>and not</u> by
                C   Ⓓ

conjunction

writing it. <u>No error</u>
        Ⓔ

2. Although <u>reducing</u> taxes may <u>seem</u> like an attractive
          A   B

proposition, <u>they</u> may impair the county's ability to
        Ⓒ

maintain services that all of <u>us</u> depend on. <u>No error</u>
               D   Ⓔ

3. The plots of Thomas Hardy's novels are <u>dictated</u> by
                                A

<u>such</u> exceptional sequences <u>of</u> coincidence that
 B

<u>scarcely no</u> modern reader finds them believable. <u>No error</u>
   D   E

4. <u>Devoid</u> of ornament, the <u>buildings</u> of Mies van der Rohe
   A   B

<u>depends</u> on subtlety of proportion and mechanical
     C

excellence. <u>No error</u>
   D   E

5. <u>Exceeding</u> a weight of six pounds, Camilla's baby <u>was</u>
   A   B

the <u>larger</u> of the <u>triplets</u>. <u>No error</u>
   C   D   E

GO ON TO THE NEXT PAGE

6. Although many single parents are fortunate <u>to have</u>
   A

   family and friends <u>which</u> are eager to help, an equal
   B

   number <u>complain of</u> inadequate support systems and
   C

   feelings <u>of</u> isolation. <u>No error</u>
   D   E

   pronoun

7. The <u>torturous</u> roads of the Alps, famous for winding
   A

   so <u>dramatically</u> that drivers unfamiliar with their
   B

   sharp turns <u>are frequently</u> disconcerted, <u>have been</u>
   C   D

   pictured in numerous films. <u>No error</u>
   E

   wrong word

8. <u>Proponents</u> of the new hormone therapy <u>advocate</u>
   A   B

   early intervention, frequent checkups, and <u>to comply</u>
   C

   with recommended <u>dosages</u>. <u>No error</u>
   D   E

9. Many people continue <u>to scoff</u> <u>at</u> the notion that pet
   A   B

   ownership can <u>significantly</u> reduce the onset <u>of</u>
   C   D

   stress-related illness. <u>No error</u>
   E

10. The <u>economic</u> cost <u>of purchasing</u> a country home
    A   B

    <u>proved</u> too great for the struggling family, which had
    C

    only recently seen <u>its</u> financial fortunes improve.
    D

    <u>No error</u>
    E

    redundancy

11. The audience of students, teachers, and fans <u>have</u>
    A   B

    <u>assembled</u> in the lobby <u>at the rear</u> of the theater.
    C   D

    <u>No error</u>
    E

    subject - verb agreement

12. Ruth Stout, <u>widely regarded</u> as one of the first
    A

    <u>proponents of</u> organic gardening, espoused theories
    B

    that <u>were</u> as unconventional as <u>they</u> were effective.
    C   D

    <u>No error</u>
    E

13. The popularity <u>of</u> a <u>recognizable</u> brand <u>will</u> always
    A   B   C

    dominate <u>its generic equivalent</u>. <u>No error</u>
    D   E

    faulty comparison

14. <u>Disputes in</u> the private sector forced top executives
    A

    <u>to propose</u> a series of alternative solutions <u>toward</u>
    B   C

    rampant insider <u>trading</u>. <u>No error</u>
    D   E

    idiom

15. Victims of the company's policy, <u>later ruled</u>
    A

    discriminatory <u>by</u> the court, spoke bitterly of the
    B

    <u>prosecution</u> <u>they had suffered</u> for so many years.
    C   D

    <u>No error</u>
    E

GO ON TO THE NEXT PAGE ➤

16. All interns wearing a Mount Sinai baseball hat will
    A   B

    receive complimentary meals and tickets to the benefit
    C   D

    concert. No error
            E

Number Agreement

17. Visitors to the ranch were invariably struck by the
              A   B

    tranquil atmosphere that prevailed despite the
                            C

    celebrity clientele. No error
             D   E

18. Louisa and Maria, both of who were admitted to
                             A

    their preferred colleges in April, were crushed when
    B

    they discovered that dogs were not allowed on campus.
    C   D

    No error
    E

19. During the earthquake, the noted bandleader's
    A   B

    treasured arrangements were destroyed without him
                                                C

    having an opportunity to salvage them. No error
                         D   E

Pronoun

20. Fully one hundred percent of the teachers in
    A

    attendance agreed to incorporate the board's
               B   C

    recommendations as quick as possible. No error
                       D   E

Adverb

WRITING TEST

Directions: The following sentences test correctness and effectiveness of expression. In choosing answers, follow the requirements of standard written English; that is, pay attention to grammar, choice of words, sentence construction, and punctuation.

In each of the following sentences, part of the sentence or the entire sentence is underlined. Beneath each sentence you will find five ways of phrasing the underlined part. Choice A repeats the original; the other four are different.

Choose the answer that best expresses the meaning of the original sentence. If you think the original is better than any of the alternatives, choose it; otherwise choose one of the others. Your choice should produce the most effective sentence—clear and precise, without awkwardness or ambiguity.

EXAMPLE: SAMPLE ANSWER:

    Laura Ingalls Wilder published her first book   Ⓐ ● Ⓒ Ⓓ Ⓔ
and she was sixty-five years old then.

    (A) and she was sixty-five years old then
    (B) when she was sixty-five
    (C) at age sixty-five years old
    (D) upon the reaching of sixty-five years
    (E) at the time when she was sixty-five

21. Women who were competing in the Olympic games for the first time in 1928.

    (A) Women who were competing in the Olympic games
    (B) The Olympic games who were where women were competing
    (C) Women competing in the Olympic games
    (D) Women, competing in the Olympic games who were,
    (E) Women competed in the Olympic games

22. My favorite uncle lived in a cabin in the Adirondacks, and it was not winterized, and he refused to move or to install a heating system.

    (A) My favorite uncle lived in a cabin in the Adirondacks, and it was not winterized, and he refused to move or to install a heating system.
    (B) Although his cabin in the Adirondacks was not winterized, my favorite uncle refused to move or to install a heating system.
    (C) My favorite uncle refused to move or to install a heating system, in addition to his cabin in the Adirondacks not being winterized.
    (D) Although my favorite uncle refused to move or to install a heating system, but he lived in a cabin in the Adirondacks which was not winterized.
    (E) Although he had lived in a cabin in the Adirondacks, my favorite uncle refused to move or to install a heating system even though it was not winterized.

faulty coordination

23. International travel has become less expensive but hotel accommodation and car rental causes the total price of vacations abroad to increase significantly.

    (A) causes the total price of vacations abroad to increase significantly
    (B) significantly increase the cost of vacations abroad
    (C) significantly rise the total cost of vacations abroad
    (D) significantly raises the total price of vacations abroad
    (E) cause the total price of vacations abroad to be increasing significantly

subject-verb agreement

GO ON TO THE NEXT PAGE ➡

24. Arguably one of the finest examples of modern architecture, <u>the reception to the Pompidou museum in Paris was enthusiastic</u>.

    (A) the reception to the Pompidou museum in Paris was enthusiastic
    (B) the reception to the Parisian Pompidou museum was enjoyably enthusiastic
    (C) the Pompidou museum's reception was enjoyable and enthusiastic
    (D) the Pompidou museum enjoyed an enthusiastic reception
    (E) the Pompidou museum was received by enjoyment and enthusiasm

25. When my grandmother designed her perennial garden, <u>she had evoked Monet's famous garden at Giverny but was not directly copying it</u>.

    (A) she had evoked Monet's famous garden at Giverny but was not directly copying it
    (B) Monet's famous garden at Giverny was being evoked without being directly copied by her
    (C) she was evoking, without a direct copy, Monet's famous garden at Giverny
    (D) she evoked, but had not directly copied, Monet's famous garden at Giverny
    (E) she evoked, but did not directly copy, Monet's famous garden at Giverny

26. A perennial favorite with teenagers and adults alike, Madonna is thought to be popular <u>not so much for her music but for her ability to remain one step ahead of the trend</u>.

    (A) not so much for her music but for her ability to remain one step ahead of the trend
    (B) not so much for her music but for being able to remain one step ahead of the trend
    (C) not so much because of her music but because of her ability to be remaining one step ahead of the trend
    (D) not for her music but for her being able to remain one step ahead of the trend
    (E) not so much for her music as for her ability to remain one step ahead of the trend

27. Katie and James had the backing of their firm's board of directors, <u>this</u> support allowed them the time and money necessary to pursue litigation.

    (A) this
    (B) consequently
    (C) and this
    (D) their
    (E) however

28. All provinces are ruled by democratically elected tribunals, <u>each with its own set of rules and regulations</u>.

    (A) each with its own set of rules and regulations
    (B) each with their own set of rules and regulations
    (C) each being subject to their own set of rules and regulations
    (D) which has its own set of rules and regulations
    (E) they each have their set of rules and regulations

29. A good translator has to be able to understand the subtleties of language <u>as well as remaining faithful to the tone</u> of the author's original text.

    (A) as well as remaining faithful to the tone
    (B) as well as remaining as faithful to the tone
    (C) and to remain faithful to the tone
    (D) and to be remaining faithful to the tone
    (E) and to remain faithful in the tone

30. Columbus discovered most of the islands in the West Indies <u>but failed to find the gold their backers demanded</u>.

    (A) but failed to find the gold their backers demanded
    (B) and failed to find the gold his backers demanded
    (C) and failed to find the gold their backers demanded
    (D) but failed to find the gold his backers demanded
    (E) but was a failure at finding the gold his backers demanded

31. Born in Dublin, <u>George Bernard Shaw's writing career did not start promisingly, failing so terribly</u> as a novelist that he was penniless for a number of years.

    (A) George Bernard Shaw's writing career did not start promisingly, failing so terribly
    (B) George Bernard Shaw's writing career did not start promisingly, having failed so terribly
    (C) George Bernard Shaw's writing career did not start promisingly but failed so terribly
    (D) the writer George Bernard Shaw did not have a promising start to his career, failing so terribly
    (E) the writer George Bernard Shaw did not start his career promisingly but failed it so terribly

GO ON TO THE NEXT PAGE

32. Neither of the two designs were chosen for inclusion in the foundation's annual brochure of innovative design.

(A) Neither of the two designs were chosen for inclusion
(B) Neither of the two designs were included
(C) Of the two designs, neither of them were chosen to be included
(D) Neither of the two designs was chosen for inclusion
(E) Of the two designs chosen for inclusion, neither was

33. By tomorrow, the principal promised, I will have had a chance to review the applications of all students who are candidates for the scholarship.

(A) will have had a chance to review the applications of all students who are candidates
(B) will have had a chance to review the applications of all students who are a candidate
(C) will chance reviewing the applications of all student candidates
(D) will be reviewing, by chance, the applications of all students who are candidates
(E) will have reviewed the candidate student applications

34. The newspaper aimed to provide coverage of current events and maintaining neutrality in its reporting.

(A) and maintaining neutrality in its reporting
(B) and maintenance of its neutral reporting
(C) but maintaining neutrality in its reporting
(D) and to maintain neutrality in its reporting
(E) despite maintaining neutrality in its reporting.

35. Determining what is fantasy and what is reality are more often the province of the psychiatrist than the prosecutor.

(A) Determining what is fantasy and what is reality are more often
(B) Determining what is fantasy and what is reality is more often
(C) Determining what is fantasy and reality are more often
(D) The determination of fantasy and reality is more often
(E) The determination between fantasy and reality is more often

36. During peak tourist season, tens of thousands of people visit the museum, which is known for its extraordinary collection of early American art.

(A) which is known for its extraordinary collection
(B) which is known for their extraordinary collection
(C) knowing about its extraordinary collection
(D) knowing about their extraordinary collections
(E) being that it is known for its extraordinary collections

37. The athlete required no additional preparation; years of rigorous training had honed her skills and maximized her endurance.

(A) The athlete required no additional preparation; years of rigorous training had honed her skills
(B) The athlete required no additional preparation, years of rigorous training had honed her skills
(C) No additional preparation was required for the athlete's years of rigorous training had honed her skills
(D) No additional preparation was required; years of rigorous training which had honed her skills
(E) Requiring no additional preparation, the athelete's years of rigorous training had honed her skills

38. I speak Italian and the job required fluency in either Italian or French and I felt comfortable interviewing for the position.

(A) I speak Italian and the job required fluency in either Italian or French and I felt comfortable interviewing for the position.
(B) Because the job required fluency in either Italian or French and I speak it, I felt comfortable interviewing for the position.
(C) Because the job required fluency in either Italian or French, and I speak Italian, which felt comfortable interviewing for the position.
(D) The job required fluency in either Italian or French, because I speak Italian, I felt comfortable interviewing for the position.
(E) Because I speak Italian and the job required fluency in either Italian or French, I felt comfortable interviewing for the position.

GO ON TO THE NEXT PAGE

WRITING TEST

Questions 39–44 are based on the following passage.

(1) *When I was younger, I thought that knowing about history was pointless; it seemed like one of those things that parents and teachers want you to learn in order to give you discipline and to make sure you do homework.* (2) *But now I know if you want to understand yourself in context of the world, it doesn't hurt to study history.* (3) *A lot of people think of Abraham Lincoln as the tall guy who fought slavery and got shot but there was a lot more to him.* (4) *He was a pioneer in the true sense of the word.* (5) *(Then again, there are definitely people who disagree and maybe it doesn't matter if you are ignorant of your past, depending on your job and how far you want to go in the world.)*

(6) *For instance, did you know that we weren't even discovered on purpose but inadvertently?* (7) *The reason I thought this was helpful to know was that a lot of other things happen by accident—scientific breakthroughs and medical advancements—and it is good to know that success can sometimes come in the midst of what feels like failure.* (8) *Newton and Gregor Mendel exemplified this principle with their persistence.* (9) *Although they weren't necessarily Americans, per se.* (10) *Consequently, knowing how hard your ancestors fought to ensure your liberty and free rights is very poignant and makes you appreciate things you could otherwise take for granted.* (11) *Once you know that the Boston Tea Party wasn't some riotous celebration but a serious battle, one looks at life differently.*

(12) *Even with the noble leaders of our past and all of the rights we have fought to maintain, our country is still very young.* (13) *Reading newspapers and taking responsibility for understanding your past in order to create a better future is the only way forward.*

39. What is the best revision of sentence 2 (reproduced below)?

   But now I know if you want to understand yourself in context of the world, it doesn't hurt to study history.

   (A) But now I know if you would like to understand yourself in context of the world, it won't hurt to study history.
   (B) Now I know that studying history can help you understand yourself in the context of the world.
   (C) However, now I know studying history can put you in the context of the world.
   (D) However, now I know if one wants to understand oneself in the context of the world, you should study history.
   (E) Now I know that studying history doesn't hurt you when you put yourself in the context of the world.

40. Which of the following sentences is LEAST essential to the second paragraph?

   (A) sentence 7
   (B) sentence 8
   (C) sentence 9
   (D) sentence 10
   (E) sentence 11

41. Which of the following would be the best replacement for *Consequently* at the beginning of sentence 10?

   (A) Furthermore
   (B) Although
   (C) Because
   (D) Despite
   (E) Finally

GO ON TO THE NEXT PAGE

42. In context, which version of the underlined portion of sentence 11 (reproduced below) is the best?

    Once you know that the Boston Tea Party wasn't some riotous celebration <u>but a serious battle, one looks at life differently</u>.

    (A) (as it is now)
    (B) but a serious battle to make one look at life differently
    (C) but a serious battle that will make one look differently at life
    (D) but a serious battle, you looked at life differently
    (E) but a serious battle, you will look at life differently

43. Which of the following revisions of sentence 12 (reproduced below) is best?

    Even with the noble leaders of our past and all of the rights we have fought to maintain, our country is still very young.

    (A) Regardless of the complexity of our history, our country is very young relative to the long histories of other nations.
    (B) Disregarding our complex history, it is still possible to see that, in relative terms, our nation is very young compared to others.
    (C) Irregardless of our history's complexity, and our noble leaders and the rights they fought to maintain, our country is very young relative to the long histories of other nations.
    (D) Only compare our history relative to other nations and it will be apparent how young we are, in spite of our complexity, as well as the rights we have fought to maintain.
    (E) The noble leaders of our past and the rights they fought to maintain make us complex, but they do not make our country's history long, relative to comparing it to those of other nations.

44. All of the following strategies are used by the writer EXCEPT

    (A) the first person
    (B) citing specific historical incidents
    (C) parenthetical clauses
    (D) point-by-point refutation of an opposing point of view
    (E) colloquial language

    ↳ informal

GO ON TO THE NEXT PAGE

WRITING TEST—*Continued*

<u>Questions 45–50</u> are based on the following passage.

(1) *Soil conservation is an important aim, which doesn't have to be expensive.* (2) *It is surprising what can be achieved in the short term.* (3) *Soil can be improved.* (4) *Its loss can be prevented.*

(5) *There are different techniques when it comes to soil erosion, but there are really just two main techniques which are used to control it.* (6) *There is either biologically based or physically based.* (7) *The most important with biological conservation is choosing the right crop.* (8) *This depends on the site.* (9) *Crops with roots that bind the soil are better than those that don't.* (10) *You have to have enough growth to ensure adequate ground cover, or erosion will not be prevented.* (11) *And ploughing along the contour can also be a key reducing factor.* (12) *Once plants are established, not only is the soil protected by them but other plants are encouraged because of the organic material provided.*

(13) *Another thing you can do is physical protection.* (14) *A battery of measures are proven effective and include terracing and wind breaks.* (15) *Maintenance is essential because when ditches are blocked, even more erosion occurs, and eventually the ground can lose its fertility.* (16) *Wind and water can be detrimental, and if vegetation does not regenerate, desert conditions can occur.* (17) *Soil erosion is a natural process, but it is important to prevent it because it can affect farming, and even urban people will feel the economic and environmental consequences.*

45. Which of the following is the best way to combine sentences 3 and 4 (reproduced below)?

    Soil can be improved. Its loss can be prevented.

    (A) Soil can be improved and its loss can be prevented.
    (B) Soil can be improved however its loss can be prevented.
    (C) Soil can be improved in order to prevent its loss.
    (D) Soil can be improved and its loss prevented.
    (E) Soil can be improved and prevented.

46. The author could best improve the first paragraph by

    (A) acknowledging the limitations of current preventative techniques
    (B) incorporating specific examples
    (C) explaining the importance of soil conservation
    (D) including more personal opinions
    (E) defining the parameters of short term versus long term

47. Which of the following is the best revision of sentence 5 (reproduced below)?

    There are different techniques when it comes to soil erosion, but there are really just two main techniques which are used to control it.

    (A) There are different techniques when it comes to soil erosion, but there are really just two main techniques.
    (B) There are different techniques but really just two which are used to control soil erosion.
    (C) There are two main techniques used to control soil erosion.
    (D) Two main techniques are going to control soil erosion.
    (E) Two main techniques control it.

GO ON TO THE NEXT PAGE

48. Which of the following is the best revision of the underlined portion of sentence 12 (reproduced below)?

Once plants are established, <u>not only is the soil protected by them but other plants are encouraged because of the organic material provided</u>.

(A) not only is the soil protected but other plants are encouraged because they are provided with organic material

(B) they not only protect the soil but encourage other plants by providing organic material

(C) they not only protect soil but provide organic material

(D) not only do they protect soil but encourage other plants because they provide them with organic material

(E) they not only protect the soil but encourage other plants by organic material

49. In sentence 13, the phrase *"Another thing you can do is"* can be made more specific if revised as

(A) Something else you can do to prevent it is

(B) Some other alternative to use is to do

(C) Another alternative is when you try

(D) There is another way which is the way of

(E) Another way to prevent soil erosion is to use

50. The best revision of sentence 14 (reproduced below) is

A battery of measures are proven effective and include terracing and wind breaks.

(A) (as it is)

(B) A battery of measures, including terracing and wind breaks, has proven effective.

(C) A battery of measures are proving effective and include terracing and wind breaks.

(D) A battery of measures is proving effective and had included terracing and wind breaks.

(E) A battery of measures, including terracing and wind breaks, have proven effective.

GO ON TO THE NEXT PAGE

WRITING TEST

51. It was expected that the scientists will continue their
            A   B   C

    research in spite of the reduction in funding. No error
                                     D   E

52. Milan and Florence, two great Italian cities, are
                                                  A

    known respectfully for their design and antiquities.
          B   C   D

    No error
    E

    101   wrong word

53. When listening to the music of modern composers such
    A

    as John Cage, the point of the work is occasionally
                                  B   C

    elusive and even downright frustrating. No error
                     D   E

    dangling participle

54. The orthopedic surgeon, as eminent as he was prudent,
                               A   B

    was concerned about me returning to work before my
                         C

    incisions had had time to heal. No error
              D   E

    pronoun

55. One of the most unique things about taking a junior
    A   B   C

    year abroad is the opportunity to practice language
                                    D

    skills on a daily basis. No error
                             E

56. He had been having difficulty incorporating the
       A

    relaxation techniques into his daily routine but this
    passed once he understood that he was under no
                                      B

    obligation to satisfy anyone but himself. No error
                          C   D   E

57. The elegant carriage and splayed feet of a ballerina

    leads to a lifetime of muscular distortion and physical
    A   B

    pain that can be mitigated, but not cured, by
              D   C

    physiotherapy and surgery. No error
                               E

    subject-verb agreement

GO ON TO THE NEXT PAGE →

58. The class was unanimous in its feeling that the
    A

    Sibelius symphony it had just heard was the nicer of
    B   C

    all classical composition of its kind. No error
    D   E

    Adverb

59. Every reader of Eliot's poetry will eventually need to
    A

    turn their attention to the extensive annotations that
    B   C

    accompany his work. No error
    D   E

    pronoun

60. Percussion instruments, which exist in widely varying
    A   B   C

    sizes and shapes, are tunable to a definite pitch and an
    D

    indefinite pitch. No error
    E

S T O P

IF YOU FINISH BEFORE TIME IS CALLED, YOU MAY CHECK YOUR WORK ON THIS TEST ONLY.
DO NOT TURN TO ANY OTHER TEST IN THIS BOOK.

SAT II Writing
Practice Test 1
Explanations

Calculating Your Score

Question Number	Correct Answer	Right	Wrong	Question Number	Correct Answer	Right	Wrong
1.	D	___	___	31.	D	___	___
2.	C	___	___	32.	D	___	___
3.	D	___	___	33.	A	___	___
4.	C	___	___	34.	D	___	___
5.	C	___	___	35.	B	___	___
6.	B	___	___	36.	A	___	___
7.	A	___	___	37.	A	___	___
8.	C	___	___	38.	E	___	___
9.	E	___	___	39.	B	___	___
10.	A	___	___	40.	C	___	___
11.	B	___	___	41.	A	___	___
12.	E	___	___	42.	E	___	___
13.	D	___	___	43.	A	___	___
14.	C	___	___	44.	D	___	___
15.	C	___	___	45.	D	___	___
16.	B	___	___	46.	C	___	___
17.	E	___	___	47.	C	___	___
18.	A	___	___	48.	B	___	___
19.	C	___	___	49.	E	___	___
20.	C	___	___	50.	B	___	___
21.	E	___	___	51.	B	___	___
22.	B	___	✓	52.	C	___	___
23.	B	✓	___	53.	A	___	___
24.	D	___	___	54.	B	___	___
25.	E	___	___	55.	B	___	___
26.	E	___	___	56.	E	___	___
27.	C	___	___	57.	A	___	___
28.	A	___	___	58.	C	___	___
29.	C	___	___	59.	B	___	___
30.	D	___	___	60.	E	___	___

Your raw score for the SAT II Writing test is a composite of your raw score in the multiple-choice section and your score on the essay. Once you have determined your composite score, use the conversion table on pages 16-17 to calculate your scaled score. To calculate your raw score, count the number of questions you answered correctly on the multiple choice: _____
$$A$$

Count the number of questions you answered incorrectly, and multiply that number by $\frac{1}{4}$:

$$\underset{B}{\rule{3cm}{0.4pt}} \times \frac{1}{4} = \underset{C}{\rule{3cm}{0.4pt}}$$

Subtract the value in field C from value in field A: _____
$$D$$

Round the number to the nearest whole number: _____
$$E$$

Take your score for the essay (ask a teacher to grade your essay or grade yourself) and multiply it by 3.43:

$$\underset{F}{\rule{3cm}{0.4pt}} \times 3.43 = \underset{G}{\rule{3cm}{0.4pt}}$$

Add the number in field E to the number in Field G: _____
$$H$$

Round the number in field H. This is your Writing SAT II score: _____

Student Essays

Total Score: 10 (each reader gave the essay a 5)

If the world is shaped by a collective of individual perception and opinion, every situation, of whatever gravity or subject, is open to interpretation. The most stunning technological advancements of the modern age testify to the fact that even beneficial discoveries have drawbacks. Similarly, the world's misfortunes can be regarded as opportunities for growth and change. Achieving the balance between finding flaws in the positive and virtues in the negative is a challenge that history has recorded time and again.

The rapid rate of scientific discovery in the last two hundred years has transformed society in largely beneficial ways. The Industrial Revolution and introduction of the railroad, telephone, automobile and aviation industries have spurred tremendous economic growth and made feasible communication and transportation opportunities that few could have envisaged. Concomitant with innovative computer technologies and the increase in trade has been a degree of cupidity resulting in egregious plundering of precious natural resources. Unscrupulous developers have laid waste to vast tracts of rainforest, and have subjected us to toxic emissions and inadequate safety controls governing new industries that revolve around energy sources and food production. The Exxon Valdez oil spill and crises at companies such as Enron and Worldcom educate us about potential corporate avarice and abuse of emerging technologies. Yet in spite of setbacks, writers and politicians such as Rachel Carson and Ralph Nader seek to protect what is now endangered, the very air we breathe, the very sun we rely on for food and warmth and life.

Just as many radical scientific and technological innovations have been shown to have drawbacks, so have many situations of political strife proved that positive change can manifest itself in the most desperate situations. Older generations often say that they couldn't have imagined the Berlin Wall coming down, or the dissolution of communist Russia. Yet even in the horror of war and oppression, new leaders emerge and there is increased persecution of despots such as Milosevic and Noriega. Aid from foreign countries foster a sense of unity; this doesn't undo the devastation but it is a hopeful way to deal with irrevocable events. The upside is elusive to find in situations of extremis, but look for it we must.

While it is indisputably true that most events can be regarded very differently depending upon one's perception, notable exceptions remain. Tragedies of immense proportions rarely produce optimistic interpretations in its immediate victims just as innovative medicines that can forestall or slow the progress of terminal illnesses aren't heralded with anything but plaudits. We must remain vigilant in determining all ramifications of each "next great thing" as it comes along—the Internet is wonderful so long as it is not abused, certain medications provide relief but should not be seen as panaceas or alternatives to a healthy lifestyle. If perspective is all, so is balance.

Discussion:

This essay was given a total score of 10 because it demonstrates *reasonably consistent competence*. The writer makes a clear argument and backs it up with fairly sophisticated evidence. The main problems of this essay lie in its poor development of the evidence and in its wordiness.

A good introduction should set forth the writer's argument and the structure of the rest of the essay. This writer does a fairly good job with her introduction. Her argument is that history has shown events to have both positive and negative sides. She mentions one of these events as *technological advancements of the modern age*, and she follows up this idea in the second paragraph, which focuses on *scientific discovery in the last two hundred years*. The biggest problem with this introduction is that it doesn't mention the topic of the third paragraph—*situations of political strife*.

#20, #53

In the second paragraph, the writer fails to show how technological advances have yielded both positive and negative results. The paragraph is full of references to "positive" technology and "negative" environmental damage, but the writer never explains the relationship between technology and the environment. The one sentence that tries to establish this relationship (the one beginning *Concomitant with innovative computer technologies and the increase in trade...*) implies a connection but doesn't explain it. The writer needs to make this connection explicit in order to move beyond superficial comments and generalizations.

The writer could have improved the second paragraph by focusing on a specific technological advance, such as the railroads, and discussing its benefits and disadvantages. She could have described how the railroads allowed for increased travel, communication, and trade over long distances. Then she could have discussed how trains contribute to pollution or how natural environments were disturbed in order to lay down railroad tracks.

The third paragraph is even more vague than the second. A few specifics in the form of dates—the year the Berlin Wall came down, the countries ruled by Milosevic and Noriega—would certainly enhance this paragraph. What the paragraph needs most is to develop its evidence. The references to the Berlin Wall, Communist Russia, Milosevic, and Noriega don't demonstrate how political situations can have both bad and good sides. These are examples of bad situations that have eventually come to an end. The writer could improve the effectiveness of the paragraph by focusing on one of her examples and showing how it has a positive side. Even if she doesn't necessarily believe that Milosevic has a good side, arguing that some of his actions could be interpreted positively would improve the coherence of the essay.

The length of the essay works in its favor. Many students, if they manage a conclusion at all, have time for only one sentence of dubious value. In this conclusion, the writer not only briefly considers a counter-argument (some events can be viewed in only one light) but also avoids repeating her introductory remarks.

One of the major failings of this essay is its wordiness. Although the SAT II Writing is a good place to show off sophisticated vocabulary, overdoing the fancy language may end up hurting the essay's score. The examiners do not like wordiness; they value clarity in addition to vocabulary. This writer crams so many long words into each line that her message is often obscured by the florid prose. You should use fancy words judiciously in your essay; those you do use will make an impact on your examiners. Also, make sure you know the meaning and spelling of the fancy words you use; you're better off using a simple word that gets across your idea than making a mistake using a fancy word.

Total Score: 4 (each reader gave the essay a 2)

It is my personal opinion that prespective means you can look at some event or person in both positive and negative ways. In my view, it is true that you can sometimes see things in more than one way, but the statement is also false because a couple things cannot be looked at in more than one way. For example, nothing can excuse war atrosities. The only prespective possible is inadequate—no atrosity is excusable. On the other hand, there is no bad prespective about someone as great as the nobility of a leader like Gandhi. In this essay I will be demonstrating when there is no prespective possible.

I will start by discussing when positive perspective cannot be used to excuse harmful actions. Such as any act that has terrible effects on fellow humans. No matter the harm or rage behind the person who causes suffering. There is nothing that can excuse violence. This is my personal point of view and some people disagree, but I think most people would agree that even if they think a war has a good end (like defeating the Nazis in World war two), the only positive perspectives about the violence of the war are weak because how can you ignore that many people die in war?

There are many examples of positive circomstances that some people would try to look at in negative ways. For example, when unemployment statistics fall, they say that is because the statistics are wrong and maybe people were retiring anyway. Or, when there is less discrimination and they drag the race riots to light. Rather than focusing towards the positive and improving society, the negative viewpoint is all that matters to some people.

In conclusion, I have shown it is possible to examine any event in either a negative or positive light. History proves it and so do current events.

Discussion:

This essay receives a score of 4 because it displays *some incompetence*. While the references to Gandhi and World War II demonstrate some ambitious thought, the multiple diction errors and convoluted ideas bog down the essay.

The writer's mistakes begin in the first line. First, the examiner knows the essay represents the author's personal opinion and doesn't need to be reminded repeatedly—or even once, for that matter. Second, the examiners won't look kindly on a student who can't correctly spell *perspective*, even though the correct spelling is given in the question.

The writer also fails to develop a clear argument. The argument suggested in the introduction is that some people and events can be viewed in only one light. The topic of the second paragraph is the impossibility of justifying war, but the writer fails to provide evidence for this assertion. The only concrete example given in this paragraph is World War II, which the writer uses to suggest how some people might view war positively—the opposite of the writer's argument.

The focus of the essay abruptly switches in the third paragraph to good situations that some people try to view negatively. The writer offers examples like unemployment and race riots but fails to elaborate on them. The whole paragraph feels out of place in the essay because it wasn't introduced in the first paragraph. The introduction should have set out the direction of the essay; instead, it focused on situations that can be considered in only one light.

The brief conclusion actually contradicts the introduction by stating that *any* event can be viewed in more than one light. Then the writer makes the mistake of saying that history has proven this argument. You should avoid simply asserting something in your essay; instead, you should use supporting detail to *show* your reader how history and current events prove your argument. Also avoid making false claims, as this writer does when she says that she has shown her argument to be true. The examiner knows that the writer has shown little and will not be encouraged by the writer's faith in herself.

Essays are graded based on your spelling and grammar as well as your ability to construct and support an argument. This writer spells poorly (*atrosity* for *atrocity*, and *circomstances* for *circumstances*) and uses sentence fragments (*Such as any act that has terrible effects on fellow humans*; *No matter the harm or rage behind the person who causes suffering*); the flurry of technical errors will hurt the essay's score.

Identifying Sentence Errors

1.   **(D)**   *Conjunction*

Kristine understands French more easily by speaking it *than* she does by writing it. To use *and* instead of *than* is to link the two ideas, not to compare them. (For the record, *and* is a coordinating conjunction.)

2.　**(C)**　　　　　　　　　　　　　　　　　　　　　　*Pronoun Agreement*

Always check the pronouns in a sentence. You may have an error of agreement (singular/plural) or case (subject/object). In this sentence, *they* modifies *reducing taxes*, which is a single activity. The question tries to confuse you by using the plural word *taxes*. But the sentence says that it is the act of *reducing taxes* that might harm the country, so you need to change the plural pronoun *their* to the singular *its*.

3.　**(D)**　　　　　　　　　　　　　　　　　　　　　　　　*Double Negative*

An alarm bell should go off whenever you see words like *scarcely* and *hardly*. Used on their own they're fine, but when they are placed next to other negative words like *no*, they become double negatives. The sentence should read *scarcely any*.

4.　**(C)**　　　　　　　　　　　　　　　　　　　　　*Subject-Verb Agreement*

Buildings is a plural noun; *depends* is a singular verb. If you're feeling nervous on test day, you might forget that putting an *s* on the end of a verb doesn't make the word plural. A slip of the eye can lead to this mistake, so check your subjects and verbs every time.

5.　**(C)**　　　　　　　　　　　　　　　　　　　　　　　　　　　*Adverb*

When comparing two objects, you should use a word ending in *-er*, also known as a comparative modifier. When you compare three or more objects, you need to use a word ending in *-est*, a superlative modifier. As a triplet, the baby is the *largest* of the three, not the *larger*.

6.　**(B)**　　　　　　　　　　　　　　　　　　　　　　　　　　　*Pronoun*

Family and friends are people; therefore, *who* should replace *which*. *Who* is a pronoun used as a replacement for people, while *which* is a stand-in for things.

7.　**(A)**　　　　　　　　　　　　　　　　　　　　　　　　　*Wrong Word*

Torturous and *tortuous* mean two different things. *Torturous* describes something that causes torture, while *tortuous* means winding and circuitous. Getting dropped from the highest peak in the Swiss Alps would be *torturous*; the winding Swiss roads are *tortuous*.

8.　**(C)**　　　　　　　　　　　　　　　　　　　　　　　　　*Parallelism*

Whenever you see a list, you should check for parallel structure errors. In this case, you've got two nouns modified by adjectives—*early intervention, frequent checkups*—and then you've got a verb—*to comply with recommended dosages*. Yes, the recommended dosages part of the sentence includes a noun, but the important part of the phrase is *to comply*. This kind of parallelism error is often made in speech, so relying on your ear won't necessarily help you catch it.

9.　**(E)**　　　　　　　　　　　　　　　　　　　　　　　　　　*No Error*

No error.

10.　**(A)**　　　　　　　　　　　　　　　　　　　　　　　　*Redundancy*

Although *cost* can apply to factors other than money—emotional cost, for instance—in this context *economic* is redundant because money is clearly the subject of the sentence. If you thought *its* sounds funny, just link it to the noun it modifies, *family*, which is one of those pesky collective singulars (like *audience, group, community*) that sound plural but aren't.

11. **(B)** — *Subject-Verb Agreement*

Watch out for prepositional clauses following singular subjects. *Of students, teachers, and fans* can draw your attention away from the true subject of this sentence—*audience*, a singular noun. If you can ignore the distracting filler between *audience* and *have assembled*, you'll see that the correct verb is *has assembled*.

12. **(E)** — *No Error*

No error.

13. **(D)** — *Faulty Comparison*

The *popularity of a recognizable brand* will always dominate the *popularity* of its generic equivalent. Alternatively, a recognizable brand will always dominate its generic equivalent. You can't say you like your labrador's hair better than your poodle—okay, you can, but not on the SAT II Writing, where you can only compare your labrador's *hair* to the *hair* of your cat.

14. **(C)** — *Idiom*

The executives want to find a solution *to* something, not *toward* (or *towards*, for that matter) something.

15. **(C)** — *Wrong Word*

If they were victims, they were suffering *persecution*, not *prosecution*. *Prosecution* is a legal term, and the testmakers were counting on you to be confused by the legal reference in the clause *later ruled discriminatory by the court*.

16. **(B)** — *Number Agreement*

Number agreement questions can be tricky, especially since you can't always count on your ear to catch the errors. All the *interns* will receive *hats*—they probably won't all share the same one.

17. **(E)** — *No Error*

No error.

18. **(A)** — *Pronoun*

Knowing when to use *who* and when to use *whom* is difficult. Many people use *who* and *whom* interchangeably, which means they use the words incorrectly. *Who* performs an action; it has the same function as pronouns like *I, she, he, we,* and *they*. *Whom* is on the receiving end of an action and has the same function as *me, her, him, us,* and *them*. If you don't know whether to use *who* or *whom* in the sentence, try substituting the pronoun with *they* or *them*. *Both of they* sounds really strange, but *both of them* sounds normal. Since *them* is right, *whom* is right too.

19. **(C)** — *Pronoun*

The object of the preposition *without* is the gerund *having*, not the pronoun *him*. The function of *him* in this sentence is to descibe *having*, but *him* is the incorrect pronoun case. To correct this sentence, you need an ownership pronoun, otherwise known as a possessive pronoun, in front of the gerund to show who "owns" the having. The having belongs to him; it is *his having*.

20. **(C)** *Adverb*

How were the teachers going to incorporate the board's recommendations? Quickly. Adverbs like *quickly* modify verbs, adjectives, and other adverbs; adjectives like *quick* modify nouns. You may have been tricked by the word *fully*, which can sound wrong to some ears even though it's grammatically correct. In this sentence, *fully* modifies the adjective phrase *one hundred*. Although *one hundred* sometimes functions as a noun, in this case it functions as a descriptive number and, therefore, takes an adverb like *fully*.

Improving Sentence Errors

21. **(E)** *Fragment*

(A), (B), (C), and (D) are not complete sentences; they are fragments. (B) has the additional problem of applying *who* to the Olympics. *Who* applies to people, not to events. (E) provides the sentence with the two essential elements of a complete sentence: a subject and an agreeing verb (*Women competed*).

22. **(B)** *Faulty Coordination*

The error in the original sentence is faulty coordination. The sentence gives equal weight to three clauses of varying significance and needs to be revised so that it demonstrates how the clauses relate to each other. (B) is the best answer choice because it shows that, in spite of the cabin's lack of heat, the uncle refuses to move or to install a heating system. (B) uses the clause about the lack of heat to demonstrate the circumstances of the uncle's refusal. Although (B) drops the clause that states that the uncle lives in the cabin, that clause is unnecessary because the sentence implies that he lives there.

23. **(B)** *Subject-Verb Agreement*

The original sentence has an error of subject-verb agreement. It is also long and clunky. (B) accommodates the compound subject, *hotel accommodation and car rental*, with a plural verb, *increase*. It also improves clarity and flow by using fewer words than the original to express the same idea.

24. **(D)** *Misplaced Modifier*

Misplaced modifiers abound in Improving Sentence questions, so you should always make sure that a modifying phrase is next to its subject. In this sentence, once you recognize that the museum itself, not the reception to the museum, is one of the finest examples of modern architecture, you can eliminate choices (A), (B), and (C), which place the museum next to its modifier. Of the remaining choices, (D) makes sense, but (E) does not. Enjoyment and enthusiasm are not capable of "receiving" anything.

25. **(E)** *Tense*

(E) is the best answer because it stays in the past tense—*she evoked but did not directly copy*. (A) and (D) jump tenses like crazy (*had evoked but was not directly copying*, for example). (C) changes the meaning of the sentence. (B) is grammatically correct, but its use of the passive voice slightly obscures the meaning of this sentence. For this question, (E) is a better answer than (B).

26. **(E)** *Idiom*

Idioms are tricky. There are a few worth memorizing, and this is one of them: *not so much for this AS for that*. When you have to consider many permutations of the same idiom, it's helpful to have the correct version plugged into your brain.

27. **(C)** *Run-on*

Two independent clauses, such as the ones in this question, should be linked by a semicolon or a coordinating conjunction (like *and*) preceded by a comma. (D) commits the same problem as the original sentence: it divides two independent clauses using only a comma. The transitional adverbs in (B) and (E) lack proper punctuation; transitional adverbs (*consequently, however*) should come after a semicolon and before a comma. Even if punctuated correctly, words like these should be considered carefully to determine how they might change a sentence's meaning. In this case, *however* would suggest a contrast that isn't indicated by the sentence.

28. **(A)** *No Error*

No error.

29. **(C)** *Parallelism*

The rules of parallelism dictate that the first infinitive in this sentence—*to understand*—be followed by a second infinitive—*to remain faithful*. By the way, (E) is almost correct, except for the use of *in* instead of *to* after *faithful*. You remain faithful *to* something, not *in* something.

30. **(D)** *Pronoun Case*

Columbus is just one guy, so the reference should be to *his* backers, not *their* backers. Always check the pronouns in a sentence, even those that aren't underlined. You need to have agreement between what is underlined and what isn't in a sentence.

31. **(D)** *Misplaced Modifier*

George Bernard Shaw, not his writing career, was born in Dublin. Once you realize that George should be the subject of the sentence, you can eliminate (A), (B), and (C). Of the two remaining choices, (D) is a better answer than (E) because it makes it clear that Shaw, not his career, failed terribly as a novelist.

32. **(D)** *Subject-Verb Agreement*

In this sentence, *neither* means none—a single entity. You need to change the verb to reflect *neither*'s single status: *neither was chosen*.

33. **(A)** *No Error*

No error.

34. **(D)** *Parallelism*

(D) is the only answer choice that respects the rules of parallelism. In the original sentence, the newspaper's aims switch from an infinitive (*to provide*) to a gerund (*maintaining*). The two aims need to be presented in the same form: the newspaper needs to provide and *to maintain*.

35. **(B)** *Subject-Verb Agreement*

The subject of this sentence is the act of determining, which requires a singular verb, *is*. The tricky part of the sentence is the lengthy clause following *determining*—by the time you get to the verb, *are*, you may have lost sight of your subject.

36. **(A)** *No Error*

No error.

37. **(A)**   *No Error*

No error.

38. **(E)**   *Coordination*

The original sentence contains three independent clauses that haven't been correctly coordinated. A correct version of the sentence would demonstrate how the clauses relate to each other. *It* in (B) is a faulty pronoun reference because it doesn't refer specifically to a noun or pronoun earlier in the sentence. (C) is a fragment consisting of three dependent clauses. (D) is a run-on sentence, in which two independent clauses are separated by a comma. Only (E) combines the clauses in a logical, grammatically correct way.

Improving Paragraphs

39. **(B)**   *Revision*

The original sentence has two main problems: it begins with the conjunction *but*, and it uses the ambiguous pronoun *it*. Choice (B) gets rid of the conjunction and eliminates the problem of the ambiguous pronoun by turning two clauses (*if you want to understand yourself...* and *it doesn't hurt to study history*) into a single, grammatically correct clause, without changing the meaning of the sentence. Choice (A) begins with *but*, so you can rule it out immediately. You can also rule out choices (C) and (D) because they illegally begin with the transitional adverb *however*. Although choice (E) begins correctly, it alters the meaning of the sentence.

40. **(C)**   *Analysis*

This essay purports to discuss the importance of knowing something about history. Although the second paragraph is a digressive hodgepodge of thought, sentence 9, which states that Newton and Mendel weren't American per se, is especially irrelevant. Parenthetical asides can be informative, but this particular parenthetical clause is irrelevant to the author's argument.

41. **(A)**   *Revision*

In this sentence, the writer is providing an additional piece of information to support his or her argument. *Futhermore* indicates that the sentence is an added supportive thought.

Although and *Despite* aren't good replacements because they suggest a contrast or opposition that is not in the sentence. *Because* suggests a causal link that doesn't exist with the preceding sentence. *Finally* implies that this sentence is the last in a series of points, but the paragraph fails to build points in any logical manner, and, anyway, the sentence isn't the last sentence in the paragraph.

42. **(E)**   *Revision*

The original sentence incorrectly switches pronoun case from *you* in the first clause to *one* in the second. (E) offers pronoun agreement (*you* and *you*) and uses sensible verb tenses. The first clause says *once you know*, suggesting that you don't know yet, so the use of the future tense in the second clause (*you will look*) is logical. Choice (D), which also has correct pronoun agreement, illogically uses the past tense in the second half of the sentence: *you looked*.

43. **(A)** *Revision*

(C) should be immediately discounted due to the diction error. *Irregardless* is not a real word; *regardless* is the correct word. (A) is the best choice because it is concise and the logic is easily followed. Be suspicious of an excess of comma clauses. It may be that you are dealing with a run-on, or a sentence with faulty logic. Comma clauses can also make it tricky to spot errors of subject-verb agreement.

44. **(D)** *Analysis*

Any time you see a question that requires you to look for an exception, tread carefully. The testmakers highlighted the word EXCEPT because they know that speedy testtakers tend to seize on the first answer that says what the author *did* do. In this case, (D) is correct because the author did not argue against anyone else's position. If he did occasionally look at the other side, he did so in a scattershot, not a point-by-point, fashion.

Colloquial language means informal, conversational language. The tone of this essay is extremely colloquial: the writer addresses *you* and talks about himself.

45. **(D)** *Combining Sentences*

(D) retains the author's statement that the soil can be improved and its loss prevented, and it avoids wordiness. (B) is confusing because of *however*, which places the two clauses in opposition. While (C) is grammatically correct, it changes the author's statement by suggesting that improved soil leads to less soil loss. (E) incorrectly states that soil, not the loss of soil, can be prevented.

46. **(C)** *Analysis*

The first paragraph should introduce the topic of the essay. Of these answer choices, (C) would work best in the introduction because it explains why the topic, soil prevention, should be discussed in the rest of the essay. Choice (A) would fit best near the end of the essay; the author could discuss the limitations of current techniques and urge further research and development. (B) and (D) are too specific for an introductory paragraph and, instead, should be used as evidence in the supporting paragraphs. While defining terms can be an important function of introductions, (E)'s *short term* and *long term* don't refer to anything in particular. Does (E) mean short-term techniques, short-term soil, or short-term something else? The essay itself doesn't discuss any time frames, so (E)'s definition does not belong in the opening paragraph.

47. **(C)** *Revision*

(C) is a straightforward sentence that provides the content of the original sentence without indulging in the redundancy of (A), the ambiguity of (B) and (E), or the overstatement of (D). (B) doesn't narrow down the different techniques to ones used for soil erosion, and (E) doesn't even mention soil erosion. The use of *are going* in (D) doesn't allow for the possibility that the techniques will fail.

48. **(B)** *Revision*

(B) is the best answer because it is grammatically correct and conveys the author's meaning. Answer (C) is also gramatically correct, but the sentence omits the important fact that ~~organic material encourages plant growth.~~

49. **(E)** *Revision*

Good writing should never confuse the reader. While you don't want to spell things out excessively and treat your reader like an idiot, you should make sure the reader follows the train of thought in transitions between paragraphs. (A), (B), (C), and (D) all use ambiguous terms (such as *it* and *other alternative*) that refer to nothing in particular. Only (E) states that you're talking about ways to prevent soil erosion.

50. **(B)** *Revision*

A *battery* is singular, so the plural verbs in (A), (C), and (E) won't work. (D) is also a bad answer because *is proving* and *had included* are different tenses, and the shift between them is grammatically wrong. (B) uses a singular verb, stays in one tense, and, to top it all off, gets the point across concisely.

Identifying Sentence Errors

51. **(B)** *Tense*

The original sentence incorrectly uses two different verb tenses. The corrected sentence should read, "It *was* expected that the scientists *would* continue their research," or "It *is* expected that the scientists will continue their research." Since changing *was* is not an option, change *will* and keep the actions of the sentence in the past.

52. **(C)** *Wrong Word*

You do certain things *respectfully*—bow, curtsy—but *respectively* shows how things are ordered. In this sentence, *respectively* shows that Milan is known for its design and Florence for its antiquities. Because the subject is plural (*Milan and Florence*), the pronoun *their* is correct.

53. **(A)** *Dangling Participle*

The opening phrase of the sentence, *When listening*, doesn't modify a noun or pronoun and dangles as a result. Beginning the sentence with *When you listen* or *When I listen* would replace the dangling participle with a dependent clause. You could also change the sentence to read, *When listening to John Cage, listeners often miss the point of the music.*

54. **(B)** *Pronoun*

The surgeon was concerned about *my* returning to work; the act of returning to work belongs to me. You may have thought that *eminent* was the wrong word, but *eminent* refers to a person and means distinguished, whereas *imminent* refers to an event and means impending or about to occur.

55. **(B)** *Other*

Once something is unique (or perfect, or naked, for that matter) it can't be considered any more or less unique (or perfect, or naked) than anything else. You're either unique, or you're not.

56. **(E)** *No Error*

No error.

57. **(A)** *Subject-Verb Agreement*

The compound subject (*the elegant carriage and splayed feet*) needs a plural verb, *lead*.

58. **(C)** *Adverb*

The class compares the symphony to every other classical composition. Because the comparison involves more than two objects, you need to use a superlative modifier (ending in *-est*) when describing the relative merit of Sibelius's work: The symphony was the *nicest* of any classical composition of its kind.

59. **(B)** *Pronoun*

Always check pronouns when they appear in a sentence. *Every reader* is singular, so the pronoun that refers to *reader* should be singular. *Their* is plural.

60. **(E)** *No Error*

No error.

SAT II Writing Test 2

WRITING TEST 2 ANSWER SHEET

1. Ⓐ Ⓑ Ⓒ Ⓓ Ⓔ	21. Ⓐ Ⓑ Ⓒ Ⓓ Ⓔ	41. Ⓐ Ⓑ Ⓒ Ⓓ Ⓔ
2. Ⓐ Ⓑ Ⓒ Ⓓ Ⓔ	22. Ⓐ Ⓑ Ⓒ Ⓓ Ⓔ	42. Ⓐ Ⓑ Ⓒ Ⓓ Ⓔ
3. Ⓐ Ⓑ Ⓒ Ⓓ Ⓔ	23. Ⓐ Ⓑ Ⓒ Ⓓ Ⓔ	43. Ⓐ Ⓑ Ⓒ Ⓓ Ⓔ
4. Ⓐ Ⓑ Ⓒ Ⓓ Ⓔ	24. Ⓐ Ⓑ Ⓒ Ⓓ Ⓔ	44. Ⓐ Ⓑ Ⓒ Ⓓ Ⓔ
5. Ⓐ Ⓑ Ⓒ Ⓓ Ⓔ	25. Ⓐ Ⓑ Ⓒ Ⓓ Ⓔ	45. Ⓐ Ⓑ Ⓒ Ⓓ Ⓔ
6. Ⓐ Ⓑ Ⓒ Ⓓ Ⓔ	26. Ⓐ Ⓑ Ⓒ Ⓓ Ⓔ	46. Ⓐ Ⓑ Ⓒ Ⓓ Ⓔ
7. Ⓐ Ⓑ Ⓒ Ⓓ Ⓔ	27. Ⓐ Ⓑ Ⓒ Ⓓ Ⓔ	47. Ⓐ Ⓑ Ⓒ Ⓓ Ⓔ
8. Ⓐ Ⓑ Ⓒ Ⓓ Ⓔ	28. Ⓐ Ⓑ Ⓒ Ⓓ Ⓔ	48. Ⓐ Ⓑ Ⓒ Ⓓ Ⓔ
9. Ⓐ Ⓑ Ⓒ Ⓓ Ⓔ	29. Ⓐ Ⓑ Ⓒ Ⓓ Ⓔ	49. Ⓐ Ⓑ Ⓒ Ⓓ Ⓔ
10. Ⓐ Ⓑ Ⓒ Ⓓ Ⓔ	30. Ⓐ Ⓑ Ⓒ Ⓓ Ⓔ	50. Ⓐ Ⓑ Ⓒ Ⓓ Ⓔ
11. Ⓐ Ⓑ Ⓒ Ⓓ Ⓔ	31. Ⓐ Ⓑ Ⓒ Ⓓ Ⓔ	51. Ⓐ Ⓑ Ⓒ Ⓓ Ⓔ
12. Ⓐ Ⓑ Ⓒ Ⓓ Ⓔ	32. Ⓐ Ⓑ Ⓒ Ⓓ Ⓔ	52. Ⓐ Ⓑ Ⓒ Ⓓ Ⓔ
13. Ⓐ Ⓑ Ⓒ Ⓓ Ⓔ	33. Ⓐ Ⓑ Ⓒ Ⓓ Ⓔ	53. Ⓐ Ⓑ Ⓒ Ⓓ Ⓔ
14. Ⓐ Ⓑ Ⓒ Ⓓ Ⓔ	34. Ⓐ Ⓑ Ⓒ Ⓓ Ⓔ	54. Ⓐ Ⓑ Ⓒ Ⓓ Ⓔ
15. Ⓐ Ⓑ Ⓒ Ⓓ Ⓔ	35. Ⓐ Ⓑ Ⓒ Ⓓ Ⓔ	55. Ⓐ Ⓑ Ⓒ Ⓓ Ⓔ
16. Ⓐ Ⓑ Ⓒ Ⓓ Ⓔ	36. Ⓐ Ⓑ Ⓒ Ⓓ Ⓔ	56. Ⓐ Ⓑ Ⓒ Ⓓ Ⓔ
17. Ⓐ Ⓑ Ⓒ Ⓓ Ⓔ	37. Ⓐ Ⓑ Ⓒ Ⓓ Ⓔ	57. Ⓐ Ⓑ Ⓒ Ⓓ Ⓔ
18. Ⓐ Ⓑ Ⓒ Ⓓ Ⓔ	38. Ⓐ Ⓑ Ⓒ Ⓓ Ⓔ	58. Ⓐ Ⓑ Ⓒ Ⓓ Ⓔ
19. Ⓐ Ⓑ Ⓒ Ⓓ Ⓔ	39. Ⓐ Ⓑ Ⓒ Ⓓ Ⓔ	59. Ⓐ Ⓑ Ⓒ Ⓓ Ⓔ
20. Ⓐ Ⓑ Ⓒ Ⓓ Ⓔ	40. Ⓐ Ⓑ Ⓒ Ⓓ Ⓔ	60. Ⓐ Ⓑ Ⓒ Ⓓ Ⓔ

WRITING TEST 2

Part A

Time — 20 minutes

You have twenty minutes to plan and write an essay on the topic assigned below. DO NOT WRITE ON ANOTHER TOPIC. AN ESSAY ON ANOTHER TOPIC IS NOT ACCEPTABLE.

The essay is assigned to give you an opportunity to show how well you can write. You should, therefore, take care to express your thoughts on the topic clearly and effectively. How well you write is much more important than how much you write, but to cover the topic adequately you will probably need to write more than one paragraph. Be specific.

Your essay must be written on the following two pages. You will find that you have enough space if you write on every line, avoid wide margins, and keep your handwriting to a reasonable size. It is important to remember that what you write will be read by someone who is not familiar with your handwriting. Try to write or print so that what you are writing is legible to the reader.

Consider the following statement and assignment. Then write the essay as directed.

"Lies are sometimes justifiable."

Assignment: Choose one example from personal experience, current events, or history, literature, or any other discipline and use this example to write an essay in which you agree or disagree with the statement above. Your essay should be specific.

DO NOT WRITE YOUR ESSAY IN YOUR TEST BOOK. You will receive credit only for what you write on your answer sheet.

WHEN YOUR SUPERVISOR ANNOUNCES THAT TWENTY MINUTES HAVE PASSED, YOU MUST STOP WRITING THE ESSAY AND GO ON TO PART B IF YOU HAVE NOT ALREADY DONE SO. IF YOU FINISH YOUR ESSAY BEFORE THIS ANNOUNCEMENT, GO ON TO PART B AT ONCE.

BEGIN WRITING YOUR ESSAY ON THE ANSWER SHEET.

WRITING TEST

Part A

Time — 20 minutes

WRITING TEST

Part A

Time — 20 minutes

WRITING TEST

Part B

Time — 40 minutes

Directions: The following sentences test your knowledge of grammar, usage, diction (choice of words), and idiom.

Some sentences are correct.
No sentence contains more than one error.

You will find that the error, if there is one, is underlined and lettered. Elements of the sentence that are not underlined will not be changed. In choosing answers, follow the requirements of standard written English.

If there is an error, select the <u>one underlined part</u> that must be changed to make the sentence correct and fill in the corresponding oval on your answer sheet.

If there is no answer, fill in answer oval Ⓔ.

EXAMPLE:

<u>The other</u> delegates and <u>him</u> <u>immediately</u>
    A   B   C

accepted the resolution <u>drafted by</u> the
                      D

neutral states. <u>No error</u>
            E

SAMPLE ANSWER:

Ⓐ ● Ⓒ Ⓓ Ⓔ

---

1. Vivienne Westwood's striking designs <u>would be</u>
                               A

  heralded for years <u>to come</u> as <u>far more</u> innovative and
                  B   C

  influential than <u>Gianni Versace</u>. <u>No error</u>
               D   E

2. Assisted living offers the elderly <u>access to</u> medical
                          A

  attention, household help, and <u>they can also benefit</u>
                           B

  <u>from</u> emotional <u>support</u>. <u>No error</u>
   C   D   E

3. The Rhodesian Ridgeback, <u>hound dogs</u>
                     A

  <u>bred to hunt</u> lions, <u>was</u> the South African police dog
      B   C

  before <u>being</u> replaced by the Rottweiler. <u>No error</u>
         D   E

4. The Peace Corps recruitment officers <u>garnered</u> an
                               A

  enormous <u>amount of</u> attention from the community as
          B

  <u>its</u> visits <u>were</u> increasingly rare. <u>No error</u>
   C   D   E

5. <u>Had</u> she only <u>had</u> the brake pads replaced after the
   A   B

  first accident, the second accident <u>might never</u> have
                             C

  <u>occurred</u>. <u>No error</u>
     D   E

GO ON TO THE NEXT PAGE ➤

6. <u>Not until</u> the aspiring lifeguards had <u>swam</u> twice
      A   B

   around the lake <u>were</u> they granted <u>their</u> certificates of
              C   D

   accreditation. <u>No error</u>
             E

7. I think ice cream tastes <u>good</u>, particularly when <u>it</u>
                        A   B

   <u>will have been</u> topped with sprinkles, hot fudge, and
      C

   <u>whipped cream</u>. <u>No error</u>
       D   E

8. Remarkable <u>developments in</u> laparoscopic surgery
                A

   <u>have afforded</u> physicians the opportunity <u>to perform</u>
      B   C

   procedures that <u>mitigates</u> much of the pain and
                D

   scarring associated with traditional surgery. <u>No error</u>
                                    E

9. The mayor proposed <u>allocating</u> additional funds for
                  A

   <u>those</u> schools wishing to incorporate programs <u>where</u>
     B   C

   <u>each</u> student would receive individual attention on a
    D

   daily basis. <u>No error</u>
            E

10. For <u>approximately</u> ten years, both lawyers, neither of
         A

    <u>whom</u> resided in Chicago, <u>were</u> involved in similar
      B   C

    litigation; they <u>will be</u> retired, however, by the time
                 D

    their cases were settled by the Supreme Court. <u>No error</u>
                                   E

11. <u>In addition to</u> his fondness <u>for</u> rescuing stray dogs,
        A   B

    Jonathan <u>has been known</u> to adopt abandoned pigs,
              C

    cats, and birds <u>of exotic origin</u>. <u>No error</u>
              D   E

12. Disregarding the excellence of Sam's <u>imaginary</u> story,
                                  A

    Mr. West refused <u>to forgive</u> Sam's earlier
                B

    <u>transgressions</u> and gave <u>him</u> a failing grade. <u>No error</u>
      C   D   E

13. A number of the crops <u>is</u> resistant to insect infestations
                     A

    but <u>hardly any</u> preventative measures <u>exist to</u> protect
        B   C

    our harvest <u>from</u> the most virulent forms of blight.
             D

    <u>No error</u>
     E

14. <u>Clinging to</u> the side of the raft, the twelve <u>surviving</u>
       A   B

    crew members from Finland were exhausted <u>but</u>
                                    C

    optimistic <u>as they waited</u> for the coast guard to arrive.
               D

    <u>No error</u>
     E

15. The tenant and landlord were <u>equally</u> aggrieved when
                           A

    <u>he</u> discovered that the basement <u>had flooded</u> after the
     B   C

    <u>unprecedented</u> rainfall. <u>No error</u>
       D   E

16. <u>In spite of the fact</u> that he has always exercised more
        A

    <u>vigorous</u> than anyone in his family, he is the only one <u>to</u>
      B   C

    <u>have suffered</u> heart disease. <u>No error</u>
       D   E

GO ON TO THE NEXT PAGE

17. <u>Our</u> mother <u>always attributed</u> the tremendous
    A   B

    understanding between my brother and <u>I</u> to the fact
                                   C

    <u>that</u> we are twins. <u>No error</u>
    D   E

18. Lawyers are <u>proscribed</u> from <u>breaching</u> their clients'
              A   B

    confidentiality <u>and, consequently,</u> <u>exercising</u> great
                  C   D

    care in discussing their work. <u>No error</u>
                            E

19. Child prodigies, especially <u>those</u> in the public eye,
                         A

    complain <u>frequently</u> of the incessant attention <u>paid to</u>
            B   C

    <u>their</u> youth. <u>No error</u>
    D   E

20. <u>After</u> significant public scrutiny, the bank finally
    A

    admitted that an <u>inordinately</u> high number of <u>their</u>
                   B   C

    employees <u>were discouraged</u> from taking advantage of
              D

    its retirement plans. <u>No error</u>
                   E

GO ON TO THE NEXT PAGE

WRITING TEST

21. Ronald Reagan was an actor in numerous films and they experienced a resurgence in popularity during his political campaigns.

    (A) films and they experienced a resurgence in popularity
    (B) films that experienced a resurgence in popularity during
    (C) films, being that they experienced a resurgence in popularity during
    (D) films and experiencing a resurgency during
    (E) films, they experienced

22. While the mechanical engineers have conducted numerous tests confirming the structure's stability, the public had remained unconvinced of the building's safety.

    (A) the public had remained unconvinced of the building's safety
    (B) the public had remained unconvinced in the building's safety
    (C) they have not convinced the public of the building's safety
    (D) unconvincing though the public remains of the building's safety
    (E) the building's safety is unconvincing to the public

23. The environmental activists took the position that the proposed plant would produce unacceptable toxic emissions, noise pollution, and job loss.

    (A) proposed plant would produce unacceptable toxic emissions, noise pollution, and job loss
    (B) proposed plant would produce unacceptable toxic emissions, noise pollution, and a reduction in the number of jobs available
    (C) proposed plant will produce unacceptable toxic emissions, noise pollution, and job loss es for many people
    (D) proposal of a plant would produce unacceptable toxic emissions, noise pollution, and job losses for many people
    (E) proposed plant would be producing unacceptable toxic emissions, noise pollution, and job loss

GO ON TO THE NEXT PAGE

24. Having an extraordinary tolerance for harsh winds and extremes of temperature, the botanists chose the cactus for their experiment on moisture retention.

    (A) Having an extraordinary tolerance for harsh winds and extremes of temperature, the botanists chose the cactus for their experiment on moisture retention.
    (B) The botanists chose the cactus for their experiment on moisture retention because of its extraordinary tolerance for harsh winds and extremes of temperature.
    (C) The botanists chose the cactus for their experiment on moisture retention being as it has an extraordinary tolerance for harsh winds and extremes of temperature.
    (D) The botanists who chose the cactus for their experiment on moisture retention did so because of their extraordinary tolerance for harsh winds and extremes of temperature.
    (E) Having an extraordinary tolerance for harsh winds and extremes of temperature, the botanists were choosing the cactus for their experiment on moisture retention.

25. The landscape gardener was stimulated by his trips abroad that modeled many of his designs after famous European gardens.

    (A) gardener was stimulated by his trips abroad that modeled many of his designs
    (B) gardener was stimulated by his trips abroad that had modeled many of his designs
    (C) gardener, stimulated by his trips abroad, modeled many of his designs
    (D) gardener's designs, stimulated by his trips abroad, modeled many of his gardens
    (E) gardener was stimulated by his trips abroad which resulted in his modeling many of his designs

26. The fields, once almost barren, are now fertile, verdant sources of food for the community.

    (A) fields, once almost barren, are now
    (B) fields, though it was once almost barren, are now
    (C) fields, due to the fact that they were once almost barren, are now
    (D) fields, in spite of having been almost barren once, are now
    (E) fields, once almost barren, being nowadays

27. Marcel Duchamp was very impressed by a visit to Alexander Calder's studio, this visit inspired him to exhibit Calder's work in 1932.

    (A) studio, this visit inspired
    (B) studio; but this visit inspired
    (C) studio, but this visit inspired
    (D) studio, consequently this visit inspired
    (E) studio, and this visit inspired

28. The belief that all technological innovations should be heralded as signs of progress dominating the first half of the twentieth century.

    (A) innovations should be heralded as signs of progress dominating
    (B) innovations would be heralded as signs of progress have been dominating
    (C) innovations should be heralded as signs of progress will be dominating
    (D) innovations should be heralded as signs of progress dominated
    (E) innovations would be heralded as progress signs dominated

29. My favorite movies depict ordinary people who face difficult moments in their lives, featuring Jimmy Stewart.

    (A) movies depict ordinary people who face difficult moments in their lives, featuring
    (B) movies depict ordinary people who face difficult moments in their lives that feature
    (C) movies, which depict ordinary people who face difficult moments in their lives and which feature
    (D) movies, which depict ordinary people who face difficult moments in their lives, feature
    (E) movies, having depicted ordinary people who face difficult moments in their lives, feature

GO ON TO THE NEXT PAGE

30. For many screenwriters, <u>having their scripts produced is more thrilling than having</u> their salaries increased.

    (A) having their scripts produced is more thrilling than having
    (B) having their scripts produced is more thrilling than to increase
    (C) having production of scripts is more thrilling than increasing
    (D) having scripts produced is more thrilling than to have
    (E) it is more thrilling to have scripts produced than having

31. Although inclement weather conditions are common, <u>deterring most tourists from visiting</u> the site.

    (A) deterring most tourists from visiting
    (B) yet most tourists are not deterred from visiting
    (C) they do not deter most tourists from visiting
    (D) and they do not deter most visitors from visiting
    (E) they had not deterred most visitors from visiting

32. Applications for the scholarship are mailed <u>to qualifying students and consequently eligible candidates who don't receive one should contact their professors</u>.

    (A) to qualifying students and consequently eligible candidates who don't receive one should contact their professors
    (B) to qualifying students; eligible candidates who don't receive one should contact their professors
    (C) to qualifying students or consequently eligible candidates should contact their professors if they don't receive one
    (D) to qualifying students who, if they don't receive one, but are eligible candidates, should contact their professors
    (E) to qualifying students, who won't receive one if they aren't eligible and don't contact their professors

33. By coercing the victim into silence, <u>the judge said that the defendant had increased the gravity</u> of his crime.

    (A) the judge said that the defendant had increased the gravity
    (B) the defendant had, according to the judge, increased the gravity
    (C) the judge said that the defendant has increased his crime's gravity
    (D) the defendant has been increasing the gravity according to the judge
    (E) the gravity had increased according to the judge

34. The royal family has always been subject to speculation and <u>scrutiny; in recent years, however, it has been suggested that the public's interest</u> is finally waning in the face of such exhaustive media coverage.

    (A) scrutiny; in recent years, however, it has been suggested that the public's interest
    (B) scrutiny, and yet in recent years it had been suggested that the public's interest
    (C) scrutiny; in recent years, however, it had been suggested that the public's interest
    (D) scrutiny, however, in recent years, the suggestion is that the public's interest
    (E) scrutiny; however, in recent years, the public's interest suggests it

35. <u>Dominating the investigation of the accident was the suggestion by the insurance company that action not be taken until the engineer would be interviewed.</u>

    (A) Dominating the investigation of the accident was the insistence by the insurance company that action not be taken until the engineer would be interviewed.
    (B) The investigation of the accident was dominated by the insurance company's insistence that action be taken when the engineer would be interviewed.
    (C) Dominating the insurance company's investigation of the accident was the insistence that the engineer would be interviewed before action is taken.
    (D) The investigation of the accident was dominated by the insurance company's insistence that action be taken until the engineer was interviewed.
    (E) The investigation of the accident was dominated by the insurance company's insistence that no action be taken until the engineer was interviewed.

36. The music course was only introductory but it offered students the opportunity to learn to read music <u>and they could also play basic tunes</u>.

    (A) and they could also play basic tunes
    (B) as well as playing basic tunes
    (C) and to play basic tunes
    (D) and to play tunes which were basic
    (E) and to also play basic tunes

GO ON TO THE NEXT PAGE ➡

37. Many French farmers developed methods of preserving fresh produce <u>that resulted in their families being fed</u> over the long winters.

    (A) that resulted in their families being fed
    (B) that resulted in their feeding their families
    (C) that enabled their families to feed
    (D) that enabled them to feed their families
    (E) that enabled their families to feed them

38. Opening his suitcase for inspection, <u>the traveler was horrified to note that his foie gras had exploded and covered</u> his clothing in imported goose liver.

    (A) the traveler was horrified to note that his foie gras had exploded and covered
    (B) the traveler was horrified in noting that his foie gras had exploded and covered
    (C) the foie gras that had exploded and covered horrified the traveler and
    (D) the traveler's foie gras had exploded and covered
    (E) the traveler was horrified to note the foie gras exploded and covering

GO ON TO THE NEXT PAGE

WRITING TEST

Directions: Each of the following passages is an early draft of an essay. Some parts of the passages need to be rewritten.

Read each passage and answer the questions that follow. Some questions are about particular sentences or parts of sentences and ask you to improve sentence structure and word choice. Other questions refer to parts of the essay or the entire essay and ask you to consider organization and development. In making your decisions, follow the conventions of standard written English. After you have chosen your answer, fill in the corresponding oval on your answer sheet.

Questions 39–44 are based on the following passage.

(1) *Ancient Egypt and Sumer were thought to have been the earliest areas of civilization in the world.* (2) *This idea lasted until the mid-19th century when British engineers lying railroad track in India discovered two buried cities who were taken to mean that an ancient civilization had existed in India as long as 3000 BC.* (3) *Villages, tribal republics and powerful states were invaded and subjected to wars, and many different empires and dynasties held power at different times.* (4) *There were many kinds of different religions, and there was a caste system that specified at least seven classes of Indian society.*

(5) *In the first several centuries of the early Medieval Period, India was always being invaded by the Middle East and Asia.* (6) *Because of its geography, India was especially susceptible to these attacks.* (7) *Some analysts even think that it was as though India was built to be attacked by other countries.* (8) *Even though the Himalayan mountain ranges made it look as though the country—at least on its northern end—was closely guarded, this was not true.* (9) *There were many accessible passes through which traders as well as invaders could travel.* (10) *For example, the Khyber and the Bolan and the Khurram.* (11) *Invaders came from central Asia, China, and from Parthia, which is now known as Iraq.*

(12) *India still produced what is widely regarded as its greatest Hindu dynasty, called the Imperial Guptas.* (13) *During the Gupta period, great art flourished in the form of painting, sculpture, and literature.* (14) *Towards the end of the Gupta period, Buddhism was eclipsed by Hinduism.* (15) *As the Gupta Empire splintered, that region of India had divided in separate Hindu kingdoms who had many names too obscure to detail here.*

39. Which of the following sentences most clearly encapsulates the main idea of the passage?

(A) Ancient Egypt, Sumer, and India were all early areas of civilization and were frequently invaded.
(B) India's geography made it especially susceptible to invasions.
(C) One of the earliest areas of civilization, India had a culture which thrived in spite of frequent invasions by neighboring countries.
(D) India produced great art which flourished in the form of painting, sculpture and literature.
(E) There were many different religions in medieval India, although Buddhism was eventually eclipsed by Hinduism.

40. Which of the following improves the underlined section of sentence 2 (reproduced below)?

This idea lasted until the mid-19th century when British engineers lying railroad track in India discovered two buried cities who were taken to mean that an ancient civilization had existed in India as long as 3000 BC.

(A) (As it is now)
(B) engineers, who were lying railroad track in India, discovered two buried cities, indicating
(C) engineers, who were laying railroad track in India, discovered an indication of two buried cities that meant
(D) engineers laying railroad track in India discovered two buried cities, which indicated
(E) engineers laying railroad track in India had discovered two buries cities, indicating

GO ON TO THE NEXT PAGE

41. Sentence 6 serves as

    (A) a summation of theories advanced in the introductory paragraph
    (B) a refutation of the theory that India was itself a hostile invader
    (C) an assertion that is not borne out by subsequent details
    (D) a logical paradox in context of the final paragraph
    (E) an explication of the previous sentence

42. In the context of the preceding paragraphs, which addition to the beginning of sentence 12 would provide the smoothest transition?

    (A) In spite of the invasions it suffered,
    (B) Despite invaders such as those mentioned above,
    (C) Central Asian invaders as well as those from China and Parthia aside,
    (D) What is important to remember is that in spite of all
    (E) Regardless of all,

43. The author does all of the following EXCEPT

    (A) allude to an old misconception
    (B) link a country's physical terrain to its vulnerability to military incursion
    (C) make reference to other historians' critical analysis of India's history
    (D) discuss a number of transitions, from military to religious
    (E) satirize the Buddhists who allowed themselves to be eclipsed by followers of Hinduism

44. In the context of the passage, which of the following is the best revision of sentence 15 (reproduced below)?

    As the Gupta Empire splintered, that region of India divided into separate Hindu kingdoms who had many names too obscure to detail here.

    (A) (As it is now)
    (B) As the Gupta Empire splintered, that region of India was divided into a series of separate Hindu kingdoms.
    (C) As the Gupta Empire was splintering, that region of India was separating into divisions of kingdoms.
    (D) As the Gupta Empire was splintered, that region of India divided into separating Hindu kingdoms with names too obscure to detail here.
    (E) Too obscure to detail here are the many names of the regions that the Gupta Empire splintered into after its division.

GO ON TO THE NEXT PAGE

Questions 45–50 are based on the following passage.

(1) *Photography is a debated subject in the art world.* (2) *Many critics refuse to recognize pictures from a camera as art at all, while other critics make a distinction between "fine art photography" and commercial photography.* (3) *Photojournalists complicate the matter even more, as do photographers who are operating in all three of the worlds heretofore mentioned.*

(4) *Many film directors originally made music video and commercials—David Fincher is one famous example.* (5) *This hasn't damaged their reputations as artists, though.* (6) *And it's not as though making this kind of commercial is costing them anything in the way of prestige.* (7) *Spike Lee directs commercials with no penalty to his standing in the film world, and famous actors do voiceovers and nobody thinks they are less good actors because of it.* (8) *Even if some actors won't do commercials anywhere but Japan, no one seems to care even if they find out and sometimes it has even made them cooler, certainly richer.* (9) *This is not the same for photographers.* (10) *When Herb Ritts took pictures of Madonna, people thought he cheapened himself.* (11) *Because he makes a lot of money, people think he can't also be an artist.*

(12) *Diane Arbus was a photographer whose striking originality was not just in her subject matter but was also evidenced in her technique which is why she is considered a major photographer of the twentieth century.* (13) *Arbus refused to accept what she said were artificial boundaries between "art" and "art for hire."* (14) *She took commissioned portraits and magazine assignments in addition to her personal work.*

(15) *Arbus studied with another photographer, also famous, called Lisette Model and first took pictures in the early 1940s.* (16) *At that time, photographers counted on magazine work to provide the bulk of his or her incomes.* (17) *Many admirers of Arbus' work don't realize that some of their favorite photographs were taken for magazine assignments but were never published in the end.* (18) *I wonder if the people who buy her pictures would pay less if they knew they weren't meant to be art but to fulfil some editorial director's "vision."*

45. Which of the following would be the most suitable sentence to insert immediately after sentence 4 ?

(A) In spite of his film career's commercial origins, Fincher has not been stigmatized in the way that many print photographers still are.
(B) In spite of his success, Fincher does not stand alone, nor is he stigmatized as Spike Lee and Herb Ritts have been.
(C) Whether or not Fincher directs commercials is irrelevant to the fact that he came from music videos and is still offered films.
(D) Like Arbus before him, Fincher overcame the unfair division between art and commerce that still penalizes prestigious artists such as Madonna.
(E) Fincher could almost be considered in the category of actors and actresses who do commercials in Japan so that they will not be stigmatized by their fans.

46. Deleting which of the following sentences from the second paragraph would most improve clarity?

(A) Sentence 4
(B) Sentence 5
(C) Sentence 6
(D) Sentence 7
(E) Sentence 8

47. In context, sentence 5 could be made more precise by adding which of the following words after "*This*"?

(A) man
(B) commercial work
(C) kind of film
(D) money
(E) industry

GO ON TO THE NEXT PAGE

48. The function of the second paragraph (sentences 4 through 11) is to

   (A) refute the claim that directors of commercials don't have the technical ability to handle feature films
   (B) penalize those adhering to the view that actors and directors should be more candid about their sources of income
   (C) conflate the career paths of directors and actors in order to illustrate the similarity of the two pursuits
   (D) exemplify the stigma attached to artists working for monetary gain
   (E) suggest a double standard between the art world's perception of commercial photography and commercial film work

49. Which of the following is the best revision of sentence 12 (reproduced below)?

   Diane Arbus was a photographer whose striking originality was not just in her subject matter but was also evidenced in her technique which is why she is considered a major photographer of the twentieth century.

   (A) (As it is now)
   (B) Diane Arbus, a photographer in whose work striking originality was seen not just in subject matter but technique, was considered a major photographer of the twentieth century.
   (C) Diane Arbus, being a strikingly original photographer in subject matter and technique, could only have been considered the twentieth century's major photographer.
   (D) Diane Arbus, a photographer whose striking originality was apparent in her subject matter and her technique, is considered a major photographer of the twentieth century.
   (E) Diane Arbus was a photographer of striking originality in both subject matter and technique, leading to her consideration as the twentieth century's major photographer.

50. Which of the following is the best revision of the underlined portion of sentence 16 (reproduced below)?

   At that time, photographers counted on magazine work to provide the bulk of his or her incomes.

   (A) to provide the bulk of their incomes
   (B) to provide the bulk income
   (C) for providing the bulk of his or her incomes
   (D) to have been providing the bulk of his or her incomes
   (E) to have been providing the bulk of their incomes

GO ON TO THE NEXT PAGE

WRITING TEST

51. What provoked her younger brother's jealousy was not
     A

the disproportionate amount of attention she received
                                      B

but the fact that she was taller than him. No error
C   D   E

52. Conspicuously present at the couple's wedding were a
     A   B

group of rowdy students and colleagues, over whose
                                   C

boisterous catcalls the couple strained to make their
                                 D

vows heard. No error
          E

53. It isn't that none of us is interested in maintaining the
                      A   B

peace but that none of us wants to force others to
                          C

comply with the rules. No error
     D   E

54. Modern readers often find the plots of Victorian novels

overly contrived because writers such as Charles
    A

Dickens, who was paid to produce a weekly serial, were
             B   C

obligated to be providing great suspense at the
         D

conclusion of each chapter. No error
                 E

55. Many landowners in the area say that they prefer to
                                  A

abide by the nature conservancy's rules rather than by
     B   C

the homeowners. No error
     D   E

56. Most new cars are available with additional safety
               A

features that are not scarcely as expensive as many
                   B   C

frugal consumers have been led to expect. No error
               D   E

GO ON TO THE NEXT PAGE ➤

57. <u>Noted</u> artists such as Jackson Pollock and Willem de
      A

  Kooning <u>took up</u> residence on the eastern end of Long
          B

  Island well before <u>it</u> became a trendy beach community
             C

  known for <u>its</u> exorbitant prices and celebrity culture.
         D

  <u>No error</u>
       E

58. Should <u>you</u> wish to travel to Alaska, one <u>might</u>
        A   B

  <u>consider purchasing</u> a down jacket and <u>several</u> pairs of
           C   D

  thermal socks. <u>No error</u>
               E

59. After the executive was indicted for fraud, he <u>is</u>
                                     A

  shunned by members of polite society <u>who</u>
                               B

  believed that associating with a convicted felon <u>would</u>
                                           C

  reduce <u>their</u> standing in the community. <u>No error</u>
          D   E

60. Combined <u>together</u> with flour, butter, salt, and sugar,
            A

  a pinch of baking powder and a <u>deft</u> hand <u>will produce</u>
                                B   C

  a deliciously flaky pastry crust suitable <u>for</u> tarts and
                                        D

  pies. <u>No error</u>
         E

S T O P

**IF YOU FINISH BEFORE TIME IS CALLED, YOU MAY CHECK YOUR WORK ON THIS TEST ONLY.
DO NOT TURN TO ANY OTHER TEST IN THIS BOOK.**

SAT II Writing
Practice Test 2
Explanations

Calculating Your Score

Question Number	Correct Answer	Right	Wrong	Question Number	Correct Answer	Right	Wrong
1.	D	___	___	31.	C	___	___
2.	B	___	___	32.	B	___	___
3.	A	___	___	33.	B	___	___
4.	C	___	___	34.	A	___	___
5.	E	___	___	35.	E	___	___
6.	B	___	___	36.	C	___	___
7.	C	___	___	37.	D	___	___
8.	D	___	___	38.	A	___	___
9.	C	___	___	39.	C	___	___
10.	D	___	___	40.	D	___	___
11.	E	___	___	41.	E	___	___
12.	A	___	___	42.	A	___	___
13.	A	___	___	43.	E	___	___
14.	E	___	___	44.	B	___	___
15.	B	___	___	45.	A	___	___
16.	B	___	___	46.	C	___	___
17.	C	___	___	47.	B	___	___
18.	D	___	___	48.	E	___	___
19.	E	___	___	49.	D	___	___
20.	C	___	___	50.	A	___	___
21.	B	___	___	51.	D	___	___
22.	C	___	___	52.	B	___	___
23.	A	___	___	53.	E	___	___
24.	B	___	___	54.	D	___	___
25.	C	___	___	55.	D	___	___
26.	A	___	___	56.	B	___	___
27.	E	___	___	57.	E	___	___
28.	D	___	___	58.	A	___	___
29.	D	___	___	59.	A	___	___
30.	A	___	___	60.	A	___	___

Your raw score for the SAT II Writing test is a composite of your raw score in the multiple-choice section and your score on the essay. Once you have determined your composite score, use the conversion table on pages 16-17 to calculate your scaled score. To calculate your raw score, count the number of questions you answered correctly on the multiple choice: _____

A

Count the number of questions you answered incorrectly, and multiply that number by $\frac{1}{4}$:

$$\underset{B}{\underline{\hspace{3cm}}} \times \frac{1}{4} = \underset{C}{\underline{\hspace{3cm}}}$$

Subtract the value in field C from value in field A: $\underset{D}{\underline{\hspace{2cm}}}$

Round the number to the nearest whole number: $\underset{E}{\underline{\hspace{2cm}}}$

Take your score for the essay (ask a teacher to grade your essay or grade yourself) and multiply it by 3.43:

$$\underset{F}{\underline{\hspace{3cm}}} \times 3.43 = \underset{G}{\underline{\hspace{3cm}}}$$

Add the number in field E to the number in Field G: $\underset{H}{\underline{\hspace{2cm}}}$

Round the number in field H. This is your SAT II Writing score: _____

Student Essays

Total Score: 10 (each reader gave the essay a 5)

Sometimes lies are justifiable. My parents raised me to always tell the truth, and, for the most part, I have, even when the truth has gotten me into a lot of trouble. But, once, I lied because I thought it would save someone else from trouble. Although some people might disagree with me, I think lying was the right thing to do at the time.

The incident happened sophomore year. There was a new kid in my class, Alex, who was always getting into trouble. He would pull the fire alarm, heckle the teachers, and refuse to do his homework. He probably spent more time in detention than in class. At first everyone thought he was really funny and that his pranks were getting us time off from class, but eventually people became annoyed with him and called him an attention-seeker. They stopped laughing at his deranged jokes, and you could see that he was growing even more depressed and withdrawn. The teachers and principal were constantly threatening to kick him out, saying that another prank would be the last straw.

As an editor of the newspaper, I have to spend some late nights at school. Often I'm the last one to leave. As it happened, I stayed really late the night that Alex found that last straw. From the window of the editorial room, I could see someone moving around on the sports field. At first I thought the person was doing some late-night laps, but then I realized he was moving too slowly and in a jerky manner. I turned off the light in the room so I could get a better look. And then I realized that the person was digging up the field. I snuck out of the building, hoping to get a better look. Finally the person finished his dirty work and began to walk toward me. I was scared until I realized the parking lot was behind me. I moved behind a door so I couldn't be seen. When the person finally passed, I was able to see in the moonlight that it was Alex.

The next day at school I saw he had dug holes in the field that spelled out an obscene word. The school was furious since on Friday the football team was playing our main rival. The game would have to be moved somewhere else. The principal interviewed people who had been at school that night, including me. I was scared because he basically implied that I could have done it. I was tempted to say something to protect myself, but I knew Alex would be kicked out if I did, so I said instead that I hadn't seen anything. Alex wasn't a malicious attention-seeker like everyone thought, he was just a misunderstood guy with no friends. I felt sorry for him, so I decided to remain silent. Unfortunately, the result of my lie was that everyone who had stayed after school the previous day was sent to detention.

Alex somehow found out that I knew about him and that I hadn't snitched. He started saying "hi" to me in the hallway and eventually we started to hang out. Now we're good friends, and he's made other friends as well. He's stopped doing strange, destructive things. He may even run for senior class secretary. I think my lie was definitely a case of the ends justifying the means. Not only did I help a guy stay in school but I also helped him make some friends.

Discussion:

The personal subject and the unsophisticated language prevent the essay from getting the top score, but the good organization and the readability of the essay help it get a score of 10.

Unless the topic statement specifically calls for a personal essay, you should try to use examples from history, literature, and current events to back up your argument. These nonpersonal subjects will impress the readers with your broad knowledge and intelligence. Anecdotal essays, on the other hand, show that you know about yourself. If you write an anecdotal essay in response to a nonpersonal topic, you'll send the message to your readers that you couldn't think of anything else to say. Since your essay is graded on the overall impression it makes, the sophistication of the content is a significant factor in your score.

Although colloquial language is acceptable, since it naturally arises from the anecdotal subject, the lack of sophisticated sentence structure and vocabulary will indirectly harm the essay's grade. The casual tone of the essay will not impress the readers as much as a formal tone.

While the writer probably should have chosen a nonpersonal subject, his personal example does a pretty good job of supporting the argument that some lies are justifiable. In the last paragraph, the writer (somewhat smugly) explains why his lie was justified: it helped Alex stay out of trouble and make friends. Although some people may think this justification is flimsy, the important thing is that the writer makes a case for his argument.

The writer does a good job of organizing the essay. The anecdote has a natural, chronological structure, and the writer sticks to it. The first paragraph is an introduction offering the writer's argument and a segue into the story. The rest of the essay is a narrative of the incident. The final paragraph is both the culmination of the narrative and the essay's conclusion—the justification of the lie.

The strongest aspect of this essay is its accessibility. Few, if any, readers would have trouble following the organization of the essay and understanding the argument. This accessibility definitely works in favor of the essay and boosts its score.

Total Score: 4 (each reader gave the essay a 2)

I agree with the statement that "some lies are justifiable" because the statement itself is correct. On the other hand, although many people have become disgusted with many of today's politicians, telling lies is necessary in some situations in order to protect somebody from the hurtful truth.

For example, in my opinion lies are only justified if you could call them a white lie. Should one tell their best friend that they hate their hairstyle, hurting their feelings and ruining a previously positive friendship? This is definitely a question you should think about, and the answer will help you see the line between white lies and serious lies.

On the other hand, if lies are not told to protect someone else, than they are totally not justified. For a historical example, a previous president called Richard Nixon broke many laws for his own gain and our country and its citizens felt betrayed. Even if investigators had not found out what really happened at the Watergate incident, our trust would still have been violated and either way it was a perfect illustration of why lying cannot be justified—because in some situations the results of lying can be damaging on a large scale.

In conclusion, if lies are told to protect someone from hurtful information then of course they are justified. On the other hand, if they are to help yourself or to hurt another person, they cannot be. Therefore, lies are sometimes justified and sometimes not.

Discussion:

This writer makes the mistake of trying to argue for both sides of the issue. On the essay portion of the SAT II Writing, always take a stance, and stick to it! Even if you agree with both sides of the issue, you should put forth only one argument in your essay. If you feel you must include a dissenting opinion, save it for the conclusion, and then show why the dissent does not damage your argument.

The opening paragraph suggests the writer will argue that some lies are justified, but he never states his argument clearly. His assertion that he agrees with the topic statement *because the statement itself is correct* doesn't mean anything and certainly doesn't clarify the argument. The second paragraph seems to support the opening statements by arguing that white lies are justifiable because they prevent hurt feelings. The writer provides no evidence in this paragraph other than the hypothetical situation of the bad haircut. Then the third paragraph abruptly switches to discussing how lies cannot be justified if they are *not told to protect someone else*. The writer gives no previous indication that he will discuss unjustifiable lies, so this paragraph comes as a surprise.

The third paragraph contains one of the strongest parts of the essay: the discussion of Nixon. Historical examples will impress the readers and boost the essay's score. Unfortunately, this writer doesn't do much with the example. The writer could significantly strengthen the essay by stating what laws Nixon broke and how he hurt the country.

What the essay needs most is a clear argument. The writer could argue that lies are not justified and save the example of the justifiable white lie for the conclusion. Using this example in the conclusion will show that the writer has thought through possible refutations of the argument and rejected them as irrelevant or insignificant.

The writer's tendency to repeat the same ideas and sometimes even the same phrases (*on the other hand*) will probably bore the examiner. The awkward sentence structure, misuse of words, and colloquial language will also hurt his score.

Identifying Sentence Errors

1. **(D)**   *Faulty Comparison*

The writer wants to say that Westwood's designs are more innovative and influential than Versace's designs, but what comes across is that Westwood's designs are more innovative than Versace himself. Westwood's designs should be compared to *Gianni Versace's designs*, *those of Gianni Versace*, or *Gianni Versace's*.

2. **(B)**   *Parallelism*

You should always check for parallelism errors when you see a list. *Medical attention* and *household help* are two nouns modified by adjectives, but *they can also benefit* is a verb phrase. In order to respect the rules of parallelism, you need to make the third item in the list a noun as well. *Medical attention, household help, and emotional support* is a grammatically correct list.

3. **(A)**   *Subject-Descriptor Agreement*

The Rhodesian Ridgeback is a singular noun phrase, but the phrase describing the Rhodesian Ridgeback, *hound dogs*, is a plural noun phrase. Replacing *hound dogs* with *a hound dog* would fix the agreement error.

4. **(C)**   *Pronoun Agreement*

This sentence makes a pronoun agreement error when it discusses the *Peace Corps officers* and *its visits*. *Officers* is a plural noun, so the pronoun modifying *officers* must be the plural pronoun *their*, not the singular *its*.

5. **(E)**   *No Error*

No error.

6. **(B)**   *Tense*

The problem with this sentence boils down to one letter: *swam* needs to be replaced by *swum*. Today the lifeguards *swim* (present tense) around the lake; yesterday they *swam* (simple past) around the lake; and in the past they *have swum* (past participle) around the lake.

7. **(C)** *Tense*

Your ear will often help you catch tense errors. As you read through this sentence, you'll probably notice that the phrase *will have been* sounds funny. The sentence starts in the present tense (*ice cream is good*) and shifts to the future tense (*will have been*), but there's no logical reason for this shift. You can correct the error by changing the future tense to the present: *ice cream is good, particularly when it is topped with sprinkles* and other goodies.

8. **(D)** *Subject-Verb Agreement*

Because *procedures* is a plural noun, it needs the plural verb *mitigate* instead of the singular verb *mitigates*.

9. **(C)** *Diction*

Programs where should be replaced by *programs in which. Where* suggests that the programs are locations, whereas *in which* describes what happens in the programs.

10. **(D)** *Tense*

The second half of this sentence (the part after the semicolon) contains a verb tense error. The future tense verb *will be* is wrong because the writer is discussing events that occurred in the past (*their cases were settled*); instead, the sentence should say *the lawyers were retired*. If you thought that *whom resided in Chicago* sounded funny, remember that *whom* is correct because it follows a preposition, *of*.

11. **(E)** *No Error*

No error.

12. **(A)** *Wrong Word*

If Sam's story were *imaginary*, it would not exist outside Sam's head. What the sentence wants to say is that his story was *imaginative*. The *him* in (D) may seem like an ambiguous pronoun to you, but it has a clear antecedent: Sam.

13. **(A)** *Subject-Verb Agreement*

A number of the crops refers to more than one crop and should be followed by the plural verb *are* rather than the singular *is*. Although you may be tempted to pick (B) because *hardly any* sounds like a double negative, *any* is not a negative word, and the construction is correct.

14. **(E)** *No Error*

No error.

15. **(B)** *Pronoun*

Two people, *the landlord and tenant*, discovered the flooded basement, so the pronoun modifying them needs to be plural. Replace the singular pronoun *he* with the plural pronoun *they*.

16. **(B)** *Adverb*

In this sentence, the adjective *vigorous* incorrectly modifies the verb *exercised*. Adjectives modify nouns, while adverbs modify verbs. You need to replace *vigorous* with the adverb *vigorously*.

17. **(C)**   *Pronoun Case*

When a pronoun follows a preposition like *between*, you need to put the pronoun in the objective case (*him, us, them, me*). The phrase *between my brother and I* is incorrect because *I* is in the subjective case. Instead, the phrase should be *between my brother and me*.

18. **(D)**   *Gerund*

You'll get this problem wrong if you think the sentence says that lawyers are proscribed from *breaching* and from *exercising*. What the sentence wants to say is that lawyers are proscribed from breaching client confidentiality, and, as a result, they *exercise* care. If you think *proscribed* sounds like the wrong word, you may be confusing it with *prescribed*. *To prescribe* means either to dictate (*he prescribed a course of action*) or to write a medical prescription. *To proscribe* means to forbid, which makes more sense than *prescribe* in this sentence.

19. **(E)**   *No Error*

No error.

20. **(C)**   *Pronoun Agreement*

You'll often hear pronoun agreement errors like this one in speech, so don't rely on your ear to catch them. Because the bank is a single entity, the possessive pronoun referring to the bank needs to be the singular pronoun *its*, not the plural *their*. Even if *their employees* sounds right to you because *employees* is plural, you need to remember the pronoun that comes before *employees* modifies the bank.

Improving Sentence Errors

21. **(B)**   *Conjunction*

The original sentence is wrong because the conjunction *and*, which links the two independent clauses, needs to be preceded by a comma. But adding a comma isn't an option in the answer choices. You need to find an alternative way to link the two clauses in the sentence. Of the answer choices, (B) is the best option because it relates the two clauses in a clear, concise way, making the second clause dependent on the first. (E) has a comma splice, and (C) and (D) don't make sense.

22. **(C)**   *Tense*

The original sentence has a verb tense error: the engineers *have conducted*, but the public *had remained*. Although both verb phrases are in the past tense, *have conducted* is in a more recent past than *had remained*. (B) has the same tense error as the original sentence, and it contains an idiom error (*unconvinced in*). (D) implies that the public, not the building's safety, is unconvincing, and (E) uses the passive voice awkwardly. (C), the correct answer, uses the correct verb tenses and gets the point across concisely.

23. **(A)**   *No Error*

No error.

24. **(B)**   *Misplaced Modifier*

Who has an extraordinary tolerance for harsh winds and extremes of temperature? The botanists or the cactus? Only (B) makes clear that the cactus tolerates harsh winds and extreme temperatures. The botanists experiment on the cactus because of its tolerance, not because of the botanists' tolerance. You may be tempted to choose (D), since it uses the correct pronoun, *their*, to modify the botanists, but it contains a misplaced modifier.

25. **(C)**   *Other*

The original sentence states that the gardener's trips abroad modeled the designs after famous gardens. You can safely assume that the gardener, not his trips, did the modeling. Both (C) and (E) fix the error in the original sentence, but (E)'s passive voice, awkward syntax, and wordiness make it a worse choice than (C).

26. **(A)**   *No Error*

No error.

27. **(E)**   *Run-on*

The original sentence is a run-on. Its two independent clauses are jammed together with only a comma between them, but a comma isn't strong enough to hold them together on its own. These two clauses could very well be two sentences, but the answer choices ask you to combine them into a single, grammatically correct sentence. In order to join two independent clauses with a comma, you need to follow the comma with a coordinating conjunction, such as *and*, *but*, or *yet*. (E) is the best answer because it puts the coordinating conjunction *and* after the comma, and the resulting sentence makes sense.

Although (C) is grammatically correct, the use of *but* confuses the meaning of the sentence by setting up a contrast between the two clauses. (B) and (D) are punctuated incorrectly. In (B), a comma, not a semicolon, should precede the coordinating conjunction *but*. In (D), the transitional adverb *consequently* should be preceded by a semicolon and followed by a comma.

28. **(D)**   *Fragment*

The *-ing* form of a verb functions as a noun or adverb—not as a verb—so *dominating* doesn't make the sentence complete. In order to turn this fragment into a sentence, you need to replace *dominating* with *dominated*. Both (D) and (E) make the change to *dominated*, but (E) is wrong because *progress signs* is an idiomatic error.

29. **(D)**   *Misplaced Clause*

The original sentence suggests that the ordinary people's lives feature Jimmy Stewart. What the sentence really wants to say is that the movies depict ordinary people *and* feature Jimmy Stewart. Choice (D) accomplishes this feat by rewriting the sentence's main clause as *my favorite movies . . . feature Jimmy Stewart* and by using *which depict ordinary people . . .* as a dependent clause describing the movies. Choice (E) is similar in structure to choice (D), but it illogically changes the verb *depict* to *having depicted*. Choice (C) may seem tempting, but it turns the sentence into a fragment lacking an independent clause.

30. **(A)**   *No Error*

No error.

31. **(C)**   *Fragment*

The original sentence isn't a real sentence at all; it's a fragment consisting of two dependent clauses without an independent clause. In order to fix this error, you need to turn one of them into an independent clause. (C) provides this sentence with a subject and a verb: *they do not deter*.

Although (B) and (D) contain independent clauses, they are incorrect because they add the coordinating conjunctions *yet* and *and*, respectively, between the clauses. Coordinating conjunctions should not divide dependent clauses and independent clauses. (B) has an additional error: it changes the meaning of the sentence to say that bad weather does not deter visitors. (E) changes the meaning of the sentence in a similar way, and it makes a tense error by using the past tense (*had not deterred*). The first clause is in the present tense, so the second clause should be too.

32. **(B)** *Faulty Coordination*

The two independent clauses in the original sentence are linked incorrectly by the phrase *and consequently*. When you connect two independent clauses, you need to put some form of punctuation between them. (B) fixes the error in the original sentence by replacing the phrase with a semicolon.

33. **(B)** *Misplaced Modifier*

A modifier belongs next to the phrase or word it modifies. Because it places the phrase *by coercing the victim into silence* next to *the judge*, the original sentence says that the judge coerced the victim into silence. (C) also makes this error. In (E), *by coercing the victim into silence* modifies *the gravity*. In (B) and (D), the modifier correctly modifies *the defendant*. (D) is wrong because its structure is awkward (with *according to the judge* placed between *gravity* and *of his crime*) and because it implies that the increase in the crime's gravity took place over a span of time (*has been increasing*). The increase in gravity, however, took place at a single moment—the moment the defendant coerced the victim. (B) is the best answer.

34. **(A)** *No Error*

No error.

35. **(E)** *Tense*

The verb tense in *the engineer would be interviewed* disagrees with the verb tense in *dominating the investigation was*. (B) and (C) have the same tense problem (*the engineer would be interviewed*), and they also use the passive voice. (E) fixes the error by replacing *would be interviewed* with *was interviewed*.

36. **(C)** *Parallelism*

If students are offered the opportunity *to learn* to read music, then they must be offered the opporunity *to play* basic tunes. The first infinitive needs to be followed by a second infinitive in order to correct the parallelism error in this sentence. (E)'s split infinitive (*to also play*) is technically illegal. A split infinitive occurs when a word is inserted between *to* and the verb. This error can be difficult to catch because it is often made in speech, but you should be on guard for the rare occasions it appears on the SAT II Writing.

37. **(D)** *Other*

The underlined section of the original sentence uses the passive voice. By using the active voice, (D) makes the meaning of the sentence clear.

38. **(A)** *No Error*

No error.

Improving Paragraphs

39. **(C)** *Analysis*

(C) is the best answer because it discusses how India's culture has thrived despite the numerous invasions the country has suffered. The essay doesn't discuss invasions of Egypt and Sumer, so (A) is wrong. The content of (B) is correct, but (B) is too specific to be a statement of the passage's main idea. (D)'s content is also correct, but (D) doesn't cover the topics of the first two paragraphs, while (E) deals only with the last two sentences of the passage.

40. **(D)** *Revision*

(D) corrects the wrong word in the original sentence—*lying* should be replaced with *laying*. A simple way to distinguish between *lay* and *lie* is to remember that to *lay* is to place something and to *lie* is to recline— use the vowel sounds of *lay/place* and *lie/recline* for a simple phonetic trick to remember their meanings. (D) also deletes the pronoun *who*, which should be used to modify people only.

41. **(E)** *Analysis*

Sentence 5 tells you that India was subject to continual invasions. Sentence 6 tells you why these invasions happened; thus (E), which says that sentence 6 is an explication of sentence 5, is the correct answer.

42. **(A)** *Addition*

The main point of the last paragraph is that in spite of the aggressive attacks India endured, the country's cultural life still flourished. (A) establishes the contrast, giving the reader just enough information without indulging in the wordy and clunky phrasings of (B), (C), and (D). (E) isn't a good addition because of the ambiguity of *all*.

43. **(E)** *Revision*

You should pay attention to capitalized words in the question. In this case, the capitalized word *except* tells you to look for something the author does not do. The author never satirizes Buddhists in the passage, so choice (E) is correct. If you thought the author doesn't refer to other historians, take a look at sentence 7, in which the author mentions *some analysts*.

44. **(B)** *Revision*

The phrase *who had many names too obscure to detail here* is unnecessary and can be removed from the sentence. (B) and (C) get rid of this phrase, but (C) makes an idiomatic error: *divisions of kingdoms* does not mean the same thing as *divided kingdoms*. (C) also contains a bad verb form (*was splintering*) and a confusing gerund (*separating*). (B) is the best choice: the tenses agree, the unimportant details are ignored, and the meaning is clear.

45. **(A)** *Addition*

(A) is the best answer because it develops the example of David Fincher to show how a double standard exists among artistic trades. If you don't see why (A) is right, try eliminating the other choices. (B) contradicts sentence 7 by saying that Spike Lee has been stigmatized by his commercial work. (C) is wrong because the fact that Fincher comes from the commercial world is precisely what makes him a relevant example. (D) makes an inference that is not supported by the text. (E) is an illogical jumble of phrases from the passage.

46. (C) *Analysis*

Sentence 6, which begins *And it's not as though making this kind of commercial ...*, can be taken out of the passage because sentence 5 states the same thing: that some critically acclaimed directors work on commercials *with no damage to their credibility*. You may think sentence 7 is unnecessary, since the passage has already given an example of a film director who does commercial work with impunity, but a second example does less damage to a passage than redundancy.

47. (B) *Addition*

This refers to the music videos the directors made, so the addition of *commercial work* would make the sentence more precise. Although you can reasonably assume the directors made money from the music videos, *money* is the wrong choice because it's not mentioned in the previous sentence.

48. (E) *Analysis*

Sentence 7 describes a famous director, Spike Lee, who works on commercials without compromising his film career. Famous actors are also alluded to, and you are told that *nobody thinks they are less good actors because of* commercial work. Both references illustrate the double standard by demonstrating that some individuals are exempt from the stigma associated with commercial work, so (E) is the correct answer.

49. (D) *Revision*

The original sentence is extremely wordy. (D) is the best revision because it clearly illustrates the relationship between the ideas in the sentence. It emphasizes the fact that Arbus was considered a major photographer of the century, and it explains in a dependent clause what made her good.

50. (A) *Revision*

The plural noun *photographers* doesn't agree with the singular pronoun phrase in *his or her* incomes. In order to modify *photographers* correctly, you should change the singular pronoun phrase *his or her* to the plural pronoun *their*. (A) corrects the pronoun agreement error.

Identifying Sentence Errors

51. (D) *Pronoun*

In a comparison involving pronouns (*she was taller than him*), the pronoun cases need to match each other. This sentence compares *she* to *him*, but these pronouns are in different cases. You need to change *him* to *he* in order to have case agreement.

52. (B) *Subject-Verb Agreement*

The subject of this sentence is the singular noun *group*, but the verb that accompanies it is the plural *were*. In order to fix the sentence, you need to change *were* to the singular verb *is*. This agreement error can be hard to spot because *group* is followed by a prepositional phrase that sounds plural (*of rowdy students and colleagues*) and because the verb comes before the subject.

53. (E) *No Error*

No error.

54. **(D)** *Gerund*

The error in this sentence probably sounds funny to you. The gerund phrase *to be providing* should be replaced by the infinitive *to provide*. If you thought (B) was a subject-verb agreement error, notice that the singular verb *was paid* correctly modifies the singular noun *Charles Dickens*.

55. **(D)** *Faulty Comparison*

The landowners want to abide by the *rules* of the homeowners, not by the homeowners themselves. You can fix this sentence by changing *homeowners* to *homeowners' rules* or *homeowners'*.

56. **(B)** *Double Negative*

When you put two words with negative meanings, such as *not* and *scarcely*, next to each other, the statement is positive because the negatives cancel each other out. *Not scarcely as expensive* actually means *as expensive*. The corrected version should read *not as expensive* or *scarcely as expensive*.

57. **(E)** *No Error*

No error.

58. **(A)** *Pronoun Shift*

This sentence shifts from talking about *you* in the first half of the sentence to talking about *one* in the second half. Because *you* and *one* refer to the same person in this sentence, they need to stay in the same pronoun case. You can correct the error by changing *you* to *one*.

59. **(A)** *Tense*

All the action in this sentence takes place in the past (the executive *was indicted for fraud* and polite society *believed*), so the present tense verb *is shunned* needs to be changed to the past tense: *was shunned*.

60. **(A)** *Redundancy*

Combined together with is a redundant expression; the correct expression is *combined with*. Redundant expressions are used often in speech, so you may have a hard time catching this one with your ear.

SAT II Writing Test 3

WRITING TEST 3 ANSWER SHEET

1. Ⓐ Ⓑ ⓒ Ⓓ Ⓔ	21. Ⓐ Ⓑ ⓒ Ⓓ Ⓔ	41. Ⓐ Ⓑ ⓒ Ⓓ Ⓔ
2. Ⓐ Ⓑ ⓒ Ⓓ Ⓔ	22. Ⓐ Ⓑ ⓒ Ⓓ Ⓔ	42. Ⓐ Ⓑ ⓒ Ⓓ Ⓔ
3. Ⓐ Ⓑ ⓒ Ⓓ Ⓔ	23. Ⓐ Ⓑ ⓒ Ⓓ Ⓔ	43. Ⓐ Ⓑ ⓒ Ⓓ Ⓔ
4. Ⓐ Ⓑ ⓒ Ⓓ Ⓔ	24. Ⓐ Ⓑ ⓒ Ⓓ Ⓔ	44. Ⓐ Ⓑ ⓒ Ⓓ Ⓔ
5. Ⓐ Ⓑ ⓒ Ⓓ Ⓔ	25. Ⓐ Ⓑ ⓒ Ⓓ Ⓔ	45. Ⓐ Ⓑ ⓒ Ⓓ Ⓔ
6. Ⓐ Ⓑ ⓒ Ⓓ Ⓔ	26. Ⓐ Ⓑ ⓒ Ⓓ Ⓔ	46. Ⓐ Ⓑ ⓒ Ⓓ Ⓔ
7. Ⓐ Ⓑ ⓒ Ⓓ Ⓔ	27. Ⓐ Ⓑ ⓒ Ⓓ Ⓔ	47. Ⓐ Ⓑ ⓒ Ⓓ Ⓔ
8. Ⓐ Ⓑ ⓒ Ⓓ Ⓔ	28. Ⓐ Ⓑ ⓒ Ⓓ Ⓔ	48. Ⓐ Ⓑ ⓒ Ⓓ Ⓔ
9. Ⓐ Ⓑ ⓒ Ⓓ Ⓔ	29. Ⓐ Ⓑ ⓒ Ⓓ Ⓔ	49. Ⓐ Ⓑ ⓒ Ⓓ Ⓔ
10. Ⓐ Ⓑ ⓒ Ⓓ Ⓔ	30. Ⓐ Ⓑ ⓒ Ⓓ Ⓔ	50. Ⓐ Ⓑ ⓒ Ⓓ Ⓔ
11. Ⓐ Ⓑ ⓒ Ⓓ Ⓔ	31. Ⓐ Ⓑ ⓒ Ⓓ Ⓔ	51. Ⓐ Ⓑ ⓒ Ⓓ Ⓔ
12. Ⓐ Ⓑ ⓒ Ⓓ Ⓔ	32. Ⓐ Ⓑ ⓒ Ⓓ Ⓔ	52. Ⓐ Ⓑ ⓒ Ⓓ Ⓔ
13. Ⓐ Ⓑ ⓒ Ⓓ Ⓔ	33. Ⓐ Ⓑ ⓒ Ⓓ Ⓔ	53. Ⓐ Ⓑ ⓒ Ⓓ Ⓔ
14. Ⓐ Ⓑ ⓒ Ⓓ Ⓔ	34. Ⓐ Ⓑ ⓒ Ⓓ Ⓔ	54. Ⓐ Ⓑ ⓒ Ⓓ Ⓔ
15. Ⓐ Ⓑ ⓒ Ⓓ Ⓔ	35. Ⓐ Ⓑ ⓒ Ⓓ Ⓔ	55. Ⓐ Ⓑ ⓒ Ⓓ Ⓔ
16. Ⓐ Ⓑ ⓒ Ⓓ Ⓔ	36. Ⓐ Ⓑ ⓒ Ⓓ Ⓔ	56. Ⓐ Ⓑ ⓒ Ⓓ Ⓔ
17. Ⓐ Ⓑ ⓒ Ⓓ Ⓔ	37. Ⓐ Ⓑ ⓒ Ⓓ Ⓔ	57. Ⓐ Ⓑ ⓒ Ⓓ Ⓔ
18. Ⓐ Ⓑ ⓒ Ⓓ Ⓔ	38. Ⓐ Ⓑ ⓒ Ⓓ Ⓔ	58. Ⓐ Ⓑ ⓒ Ⓓ Ⓔ
19. Ⓐ Ⓑ ⓒ Ⓓ Ⓔ	39. Ⓐ Ⓑ ⓒ Ⓓ Ⓔ	59. Ⓐ Ⓑ ⓒ Ⓓ Ⓔ
20. Ⓐ Ⓑ ⓒ Ⓓ Ⓔ	40. Ⓐ Ⓑ ⓒ Ⓓ Ⓔ	60. Ⓐ Ⓑ ⓒ Ⓓ Ⓔ

WRITING TEST 3

Part A

Time — 20 minutes

You have twenty minutes to plan and write an essay on the topic assigned below. DO NOT WRITE ON ANOTHER TOPIC. AN ESSAY ON ANOTHER TOPIC IS NOT ACCEPTABLE.

The essay is assigned to give you an opportunity to show how well you can write. You should, therefore, take care to express your thoughts on the topic clearly and effectively. How well you write is much more important than how much you write, but to cover the topic adequately you will probably need to write more than one paragraph. Be specific.

Your essay must be written on the following two pages. You will find that you have enough space if you write on every line, avoid wide margins, and keep your handwriting to a reasonable size. It is important to remember that what you write will be read by someone who is not familiar with your handwriting. Try to write or print so that what you are writing is legible to the reader.

> Consider the following statement and assignment. Then write the essay as directed.
>
> "Adversity makes you stronger."
>
> Assignment: Choose one example from personal experience, current events, or history, literature, or any other discipline and use this example to write an essay in which you agree or disagree with the statement above. Your essay should be specific.

DO NOT WRITE YOUR ESSAY IN YOUR TEST BOOK. You will receive credit only for what you write on your answer sheet.

WHEN YOUR SUPERVISOR ANNOUNCES THAT TWENTY MINUTES HAVE PASSED, YOU MUST STOP WRITING THE ESSAY AND GO ON TO PART B IF YOU HAVE NOT ALREADY DONE SO. IF YOU FINISH YOUR ESSAY BEFORE THIS ANNOUNCEMENT, GO ON TO PART B AT ONCE.

BEGIN WRITING YOUR ESSAY ON THE ANSWER SHEET.

WRITING TEST

Part A

Time — 20 minutes

WRITING TEST

Part A

Time — 20 minutes

WRITING TEST

Part B

Time — 40 minutes

Directions: The following sentences test your knowledge of grammar, usage, diction (choice of words), and idiom.

Some sentences are correct.
No sentence contains more than one error.

You will find that the error, if there is one, is underlined and lettered. Elements of the sentence that are not underlined will not be changed. In choosing answers, follow the requirements of standard written English.

If there is an error, select the <u>one underlined part</u> that must be changed to make the sentence correct and fill in the corresponding oval on your answer sheet.

If there is no answer, fill in answer oval Ⓔ.

EXAMPLE:

<u>The other</u> delegates and <u>him</u> <u>immediately</u>
    A   B   C

accepted the resolution <u>drafted by</u> the
                           D

neutral states. <u>No error</u>
            E

SAMPLE ANSWER:

Ⓐ ● Ⓒ Ⓓ Ⓔ

---

1. Neither my parents nor my sister <u>are</u> going <u>to agree to</u>
                         A   B

drive me <u>into</u> the city, <u>regardless</u> of the urgency of my
        C   D

request. <u>No error</u>
        E

2. <u>You</u> will benefit <u>from</u> traveling if <u>one</u> allows oneself
  A   B   C

time <u>to adjust</u> on arrival. <u>No error</u>
     D   E

3. Asia's size, in <u>sheer</u> land mass <u>as well as</u> population, is
             A   B

<u>significantly</u> larger than <u>Europe</u>. <u>No error</u>
  C   D   E

4. The graffiti, as large <u>as it was</u> obscene, <u>had</u>
               A   B

<u>barely</u> been removed from the subway cars before the
  C

vandals <u>struck</u> again. <u>No error</u>
       D   E

5. <u>Due to</u> a lack of funding, the library <u>will no longer</u> offer
  A   B

extended hours, microfilm services, or <u>helping</u> new
                             C

cardholders <u>navigating</u> the stacks. <u>No error</u>
        D   E

GO ON TO THE NEXT PAGE ➜

6. One <u>would</u> think that even the least <u>discriminating</u>
      A   B

   viewer <u>would have been</u> able to tell that the sitcom
              C

   was the <u>dumber</u> of its kind. <u>No error</u>
          D   E

7. Contrary to popular opinion, <u>many of the most</u>
                              A

   addictive behaviors <u>are</u> not limited to <u>impoverished</u>
                   B   C

   individuals living in <u>urbane</u> environments. <u>No error</u>
                  D   E

8. Each student working <u>in</u> the library <u>must</u> remember
                   A   B

   <u>to</u> collect <u>their</u> belongings at the end of the day.
   C   D

   <u>No error</u>
     E

9. <u>When</u> you write, persistence, <u>in addition to</u> skill, <u>are</u> of
   A   B   C

   <u>paramount</u> importance. <u>No error</u>
     D   E

10. While in the <u>employ of</u> Francis I of France, Cellini <u>cast</u>
              A   B

   some of the <u>most</u> famous bronzes <u>of</u> the Renaissance
              C   D

   period. <u>No error</u>
         E

11. After <u>it</u> <u>has been</u> left fallow for many years, the ground
       A   B

   must be reconditioned before <u>they</u> can plant <u>crops</u>.
                            C   D

   <u>No error</u>
     E

12. In order to <u>have graded</u> the term papers <u>in</u> time for the
              A   B

   midwinter break, Professor Falco <u>would</u> have had to
                              C

   <u>have</u> stayed up all night. <u>No error</u>
   D   E

13. Scientists <u>established</u> the geological time-scale
           A

   <u>through</u> <u>carefully</u> study <u>of</u> sedimentary rocks and
     B   C   D

   fossils. <u>No error</u>
         E

14. <u>Almost</u> five million people in Natal <u>that speak</u> that
   A   B

   language, <u>one</u> of the <u>major</u> Bantu languages in
           C   D

   southern Africa. <u>No error</u>
              E

15. Delayed <u>by</u> circumstances beyond his control, Godfrey
        A

   was <u>nonetheless</u> concerned that his bosses would
        B

   think <u>he</u> was <u>lazy</u>. <u>No error</u>
       C   D   E

16. <u>More</u> than one member of the press commented <u>on</u> the
   A   B

   prince's striking resemblance <u>to</u> his <u>famously</u>
                        C   D

   fashionable mother. <u>No error</u>
                E

17. The wetsuits <u>were</u> designed to cling to the body
            A

   without <u>constraining</u> or <u>to hinder</u> it <u>in any way</u>.
         B   C   D

   <u>No error</u>
     E

18. While <u>dissembling</u> the table <u>prior to</u> its delivery to the
        A   B

   governor's compound, the <u>agents</u> were stunned to
                      C

   discover a <u>cache of</u> covert listening devices. <u>No error</u>
           D   E

GO ON TO THE NEXT PAGE →

19. <u>Hoping</u> to indulge <u>their</u> fondness for imported
    A   B

chocolates, Katie and Amanda, along with Barbara and

Mary, <u>paid</u> a visit <u>at</u> the Godiva shop. <u>No error</u>
     C   D   E

20. <u>Being</u> raised in a large city <u>not known</u> for calm or quiet,
    A   B

she chose <u>to attend</u> a small college <u>located in</u> a bucolic
         C   D

setting. <u>No error</u>
       E

GO ON TO THE NEXT PAGE

WRITING TEST

21. Plutonium, a radioactive element, was first obtained in 1940 through scientific experiment, and since then it will be found in trace amounts in nature.

    (A) was first obtained in 1940 through scientific experiment, and since then it will be found in trace amounts in nature
    (B) was first obtained in 1940 through scientific experiments found in trace amounts in nature
    (C) first obtained in 1940 through scientific experiment that will have been found in trace amounts in nature
    (D) was first obtained in 1940 through scientific experiment, and since then it has been found in trace amounts in nature
    (E) was, in 1940, first obtained through scientific experiment, and since then they will be found in trace amounts in nature

22. Opening up Siberia and advancing Russian interest in East Asia, the Trans-Siberian railroad extended from Moscow to the Sea of Japan.

    (A) the Trans-Siberian railroad extended from
    (B) the Trans-Siberian railroad was extended from
    (C) the Trans-Siberian railroad had been extended from
    (D) extending the Trans-Siberian railroad from
    (E) extensions of the Trans-Siberian railroad from

23. Significant changes to the menu have been made by the new chef since his arrival at the restaurant.

    (A) Significant changes to the menu have been made by the new chef
    (B) Significant changes to the menu has been made by the new chef
    (C) The menu's significant changes, made by the new chef,
    (D) The new chef has made significant changes to the menu
    (E) The new chef makes significant changes to the menu

GO ON TO THE NEXT PAGE ➤

24. Competing with newly industrialized countries such as Brazil and Korea, the balance of world trade is experiencing shifts in older and more economically established countries.

   (A) Competing with newly industrialized countries such as Brazil and Korea, the balance of world trade is experiencing shifts in older and more economically established countries.
   (B) Competing with newly industrialized countries such as Brazil and Korea, the balance of world trade will have been experiencing shifts in older and more economically established countries.
   (C) Competing with newly industrialized countries, such as Brazil and Korea, the balance of world trade, experiencing shifts, is in older and more economically established countries.
   (D) Competing with newly industrialized countries such as Brazil and Korea, older and more economically stable countries, regarding the balance of world trade, experienced shifts.
   (E) Competing with newly industrialized countries such as Brazil and Korea, older and more economically stable countries are experiencing shifts in the balance of world trade.

25. The extinction of animal species is a natural part of evolution, but in the last century we have been endangering and we do destroy species faster than they are being replaced.

   (A) we do destroy species faster
   (B) we are destroying faster species
   (C) destroying species faster
   (D) we are destructive of species faster
   (E) being destructive of species faster

26. Prior to suffering the illness that grievously impaired his hearing, Peter playing every instrument of the baroque period.

   (A) Peter playing every instrument of the baroque period
   (B) Peter has been playing every instrument of the baroque period
   (C) Peter played every instrument of the baroque period
   (D) Peter, who had been playing every instrument of the baroque period
   (E) Peter has played every instrument of the baroque period

27. Confining animals to zoos is more often a source of controversy than to keep domestic animals such as dogs and cats.

   (A) often a source of controversy than to keep domestic animals such as
   (B) often a source of controversy than to keep domestic animals like
   (C) often a controversial source than keeping domestic animals like
   (D) often a controversial source than keeping domestic animals such as
   (E) often a source of controversy than keeping domestic animals such as

28. To carry off successfully a melodramatic scene, an actor must avoid making crude emotional appeals to the audience.

   (A) an actor must avoid making crude emotional appeals
   (B) an actor must avoid making crude, albeit emotional, appeals
   (C) an actor must be avoiding crude emotional appeals
   (D) an actor had to be avoiding crude emotional appeals
   (E) actors must have made crude emotional appeals

29. Woodrow Wilson's plan for the formation of the League of Nations was crucial in international negotiations at the end of the war, but they faced much political opposition.

   (A) the end of the war, but they faced much political opposition
   (B) the end of the war, but they faced a lot of political opposition
   (C) the war's end, but they faced much political opposition
   (D) the end of the war, but it faced much political opposition
   (E) the end of the war, but it faces political opposition

GO ON TO THE NEXT PAGE

30. When the broker who sold the house died shortly after closing the deal, no one knew <u>who the new owners should address their complaint to</u>.

    (A) who the new owners should address their complaint to
    (B) who the new owners should be addressing their complaint to
    (C) to who the new owners should be addressing their complaint
    (D) to whom the new owners should address his complaint
    (E) to whom the new owners should address their complaint

31. She had had trouble remembering the security combination in the past and <u>had always relied on him having written it in her notebook in case she forgot it</u>.

    (A) had always relied on him having written it in her notebook in case she forgot it
    (B) always relied on him writing it in her notebook in case she had forgotten it
    (C) had always relied on his having written it in her notebook in case she forgot it
    (D) was always relying on him having written it in her notebook in case she forgot it
    (E) had always relied on his having written it in her notebook in case she forgets it

32. In order to train for the marathon, he <u>embarked on a strenuous program of exercise, revised his diet, and changed</u> his sleep cycle.

    (A) embarked on a strenuous program of exercise, revised his diet, and changed
    (B) embarked on a strenuous program of exercise, revised his diet, and was making changes to
    (C) had embarked on a strenuous program of exercise, revised his diet, and would make changes to
    (D) had embarked on a strenuous program of exercise, did some dieting, and worked to change
    (E) had to embark on a strenuous program of exercise, had to revise his diet, and changed

33. Outraged by her student's indiscriminate use of her expensive oil paints, <u>the artist rescinded her offer to share her supplies</u>.

    (A) the artist rescinded her offer to share her supplies
    (B) the artist rescinded her offer of sharing her supplies
    (C) the artist had rescinded her offer of sharing her supplies
    (D) the artist rescinded her offer that she would share supplies
    (E) the artist's offer to share supplies was rescinded

34. Unionist politicians dominated Northern Ireland after the rest of Ireland gained <u>its independence in 1920, to this day they still represent the region</u>.

    (A) its independence in 1920, to this day they still represent the region
    (B) its independence in 1920; to this day they still represent the region
    (C) its independence in 1920, representing the region to this day
    (D) their independence in 1920; to this day still representing the region
    (E) their independence in 1920, even though to this day they still represent the region

35. George Bernard Shaw <u>was as famous for his thinly disguised political diatribes than he was for</u> his misogynistic attitudes.

    (A) was as famous for his thinly disguised political diatribes than he was for
    (B) being as famous for his thinly disguised political diatribes than he was for
    (C) was as famous for his thinly disguised political diatribes as he was for
    (D) was as famous for his thinly disguised political diatribes than for
    (E) was famous as his thinly disguised political diatribes than he was for

GO ON TO THE NEXT PAGE

36. Stravinksy was especially fascinated by the idioms of Western music, he sought inspiration in an eclectic set of musical heritages.

(A) Stravinsky was especially fascinated by the idioms of Western music, he sought inspiration in an eclectic set of musical heritages.
(B) Stravinsky, who sought inspiration in an eclectic set of musical heritages, was especially fascinated by the idioms of Western music.
(C) Especially fascinated by the idioms of Western music, Stravinsky, who sought inspiration in an eclectic set of musical heritages.
(D) Especially fascinated by the idioms of Western music, Stravinsky seeks inspiration in an eclectic set of musical heritages.
(E) Especially fascinated by the idioms of Western music, who Stravinsky spoke of having sought inspiration in.

37. When the tree was chopped down by Alex, he feared injuring one of the spectators who had insisted on advancing beyond the boundary established by the forest ranger.

(A) When the tree was chopped down by Alex
(B) When the tree had been chopped down by Alex
(C) When Alex has chopped down the tree
(D) When Alex had been chopping down the tree
(E) When Alex chopped down the tree

38. Verbal dexterity, in addition to reading and writing skills, are an important quality in an editor.

(A) are an important quality in an editor
(B) are an important quality of an editor
(C) are important qualities of an editor
(D) is an important quality on an editor
(E) is an important quality of an editor

GO ON TO THE NEXT PAGE

WRITING TEST

Directions: Each of the following passages is an early draft of an essay. Some parts of the passages need to be rewritten.

Read each passage and answer the questions that follow. Some questions are about particular sentences or parts of sentences and ask you to improve sentence structure and word choice. Other questions refer to parts of the essay or the entire essay and ask you to consider organization and development. In making your decisions, follow the conventions of standard written English. After you have chosen your answer, fill in the corresponding oval on your answer sheet.

Questions 39–44 are based on the following passage.

(1) *Why people travel varies, of course.* (2) *Many famous travel writers have come up with a variety of reasons why.* (3) *Farthering communication between nations is just one of those.* (4) *In my personal opinion, the key ingredient the writers leave out is pleasure and escape from daily life.* (5) *Of course it is nice to see great cities and practice language skills and even be part of a bridge between nationalities, but for many of us these remain lofty goals that only make us feel inadequate.*

(6) *Technically, I don't even remember my first trip being as my mother was pregnant with me at the time.* (7) *But when we lived in Spain, I made a lot of memories, and some of my best friends are still from there.* (8) *The things I remember about Spain aren't just the cultural treasures but the food (paella my favorite!) and the feeling I have sometimes when I remember that what seems important in my new life wouldn't have been so important in Madrid.* (9) *For instance, education is important but in Madrid people don't judge you as much on how fancy your school is.* (10) *On other trips I have made, it has been interesting to see how much wealthier America is in comparison to many countries.* (11) *Sitting in my living room and looking at pictures of poor countries in a book didn't prepare me for the shock of visiting poor countries and realizing many people there didn't have real houses, let alone living rooms or fancy books.*

(12) *My point is that people travel for different reasons.* (13) *International travel has become more affordable.* (14) *Many people can now travel for pleasure as well as for business, and they can visit countries all over the world*

39. Which of the following is the best revision of sentence 1 (reproduced below)?

    Why people travel varies, of course.

    (A) People travel for a variety of reasons.
    (B) Of course people travel for a variety of motivations.
    (C) For a variety of reasons, travel included, people vary of course.
    (D) A variety of reasons determine people's motivations for travel.
    (E) People's travel varies.

40. Which of the following revisions of the underlined portion of sentence 3 (reproduced below) is best?

    Farthering communication between nations is just one of those.

    (A) Farthering communication of
    (B) Farthering communication between the
    (C) Facilitating communication in
    (D) Facilitating communication between
    (E) Fabricating communication between

GO ON TO THE NEXT PAGE

41. In context, which of the following versions of sentence 6 (reproduced below) works best?

    Technically I don't even remember my first trip abroad, being as my mother was pregnant with me at the time.

    (A) (As it is)
    (B) I don't even remember my first trip abroad since, technically, my mother was pregnant with me at the time.
    (C) I don't even remember my first trip abroad technically, being as my mother was still pregnant with me at the time.
    (D) Technically, my mother was pregnant at the time of my first trip abroad.
    (E) Technically, my first trip abroad being when my mother was pregnant, which is why I don't even remember it.

42. The function of sentence 11 is to

    (A) substantiate the author's point that individuals travel for different reasons
    (B) argue that countries are equal
    (C) give an example of the disparity between countries
    (D) highlight the contrast between his own argument and those of other travel writers
    (E) undermine the central tenet of the essay

43. Which of the following is the best combination of sentences 13 and 14 (reproduced below)?

    International travel has become more affordable. Many people can now travel for pleasure as well as for business, and they can visit countries all over the world.

    (A) Despite the affordability of international travel, many people can travel for pleasure as well as for business to countries all over the world.
    (B) Because many people now travel for pleasure as well as for business, international travel has become more affordable, and people can visit countries all over the world.
    (C) Since the cost of international travel has decreased, many people can now afford to travel for pleasure as well as business to countries all over the world.
    (D) The cost of international travel has fallen, as a result many people can now afford to travel for pleasure to countries worldwide.
    (E) The falling prices of international travel has given many people the opportunity of traveling to countries all over the world.

44. The author's style can best be described as

    (A) formal
    (B) anecdotal
    (C) alternating argument and counterargument
    (D) didactic
    (E) relying heavily on data

GO ON TO THE NEXT PAGE

Questions 45–50 are based on the following passage.

(1) *In recent years, organic gardening has received a lot of attention.* (2) *Many customers are willing to pay more for fruit and vegetables that have been grown without the use of pesticides and chemical fertilizers.* (3) *Some unscrupulous merchandisers have even profited by charging organic prices for produce grown by conventional methods.* (4) *Government controls have been put in place to help to begin to control this and, as with every new enterprise, new regulations will take time to take effect.* (5) *But organic gardening is definitely worth the extra time and expense.*

(6) *They haven't proved that pesticides such as are used on corn and strawberries are carenogenic.* (7) *There was even a big study recently that was very controversial as it proved that there is no cancer cluster on Long Island.* (8) *This in spite of many hundreds of millions of dollars being spent to prove the raised incidence of breast cancer is because of excess use of chemicals.* (9) *However, whether you believe chemicals and chemically engineered foods are dangerous or not, it can't hurt to wash your fruit and vegetables.* (10) *If you can't afford organic produce which is admittedly more expensive for a number of reasons, among them the extra loss of produce due to spoilage and insects that could have been retarded with sprays, you can have melons and bananas.* (11) *Thick-skinned fruits are considered safer, as is peeling the skin from apples and potatoes.* (12) *The downside of peeling is that you lose many of the essential nutrients which are on the top layer.*

(13) *Something else to consider when buying produce is its country of origin.* (14) *Even if you are not buying organic, you might want to wash berries from other countries with extra diligence.* (15) *Not only are other countries sometimes less vigilant about pesticide controls, they can also be less vigilant about ensuring that their exported produce isn't contaminated with E coli and other unsafe bacteria that can be transported on melon and even transferred into your fruit when you slice it open.*

45. Which pair of sentences is the LEAST essential to the essay?

(A) sentences 1 and 2
(B) sentences 2 and 3
(C) sentences 3 and 4
(D) sentences 4 and 5
(E) sentences 1 and 5

46. Which of the following is the best revision of sentence 4 (reproduced below)?

Government controls have been put in place to help to begin to control this and, as with every new enterprise, new regulations will take time to take effect.

(A) Government controls, put in place to help to begin this, will take time to take effect.
(B) Government controls have been established, but the effect of the new regulations will not be immediate.
(C) Government controls, established in place to control this, will not be immediate.
(D) Immediate though they are not, government controls are in place to begin to control this enterprise.
(E) As with every new enterprise, new regulations will take time to take effect.

GO ON TO THE NEXT PAGE

47. Which of the following revisions of sentence 10 (reproduced below) is best?

If you can't afford organic produce which is admittedly more expensive for a number of reasons, among them the extra loss of produce due to spoilage and insects that could have been retarded with sprays, you can have melons and bananas.

(A) Unfortunately, organic produce is often spoiled by insects and can cost more money; you can have melons and bananas.

(B) Organic produce is often spoiled by insects, costing more money; due to this, you can have melons and bananas, relatively cheap and safe alternatives.

(C) Due to admittedly more expensive organic produce, among them the extra losses due to spoilage, bananas and melons are cheaper.

(D) Due to increased spoilage and infestation, organic produce is often expensive; melons and bananas are cheap, relatively safe alternatives.

(E) Unable to resist spoilage and infestation without chemical sprays and pesticides, organic farmers are forced to charge more, which is why melons and bananas can be cheap, relatively safe alternatives.

48. The purpose of sentence 13 is

(A) to instruct
(B) to reprimand
(C) to emphasize
(D) to augment an earlier argument
(E) to illustrate the author's objectivity

49. The author does all of the following in this essay EXCEPT

(A) directly address the reader
(B) cite specific health hazards associated with particular kinds of produce
(C) promote organic gardening
(D) invoke environmentalists whose work has been instrumental in popularizing organic pest controls
(E) take a pragmatic rather than radical approach to analyzing current data that could be used to counter his argument

50. For the sake of concision, sentence 15 should end after the word:

(A) melon
(B) bacteria
(C) transferred
(D) fruit
(E) it

GO ON TO THE NEXT PAGE

WRITING TEST

51. The crowd of boisterous children and tired teachers,

    hungry after a cycling expedition of over a hundred
    A

    miles, were greeted with enthusiasm by the
          B   C

    restaurant's owners. No error
    D   E

52. Just as travelers vary in his or her willingness to
                              A

    accept alternate vacation dates, so do holiday resorts
                                    B

    vary in the flexibility of their cancellation policies.
    C   D

    No error
    E

53. She seemed resigned to the fact that after the birth of
                A

    the puppies she would have hardly no time to complete
                              B   C

    the research for her dissertation. No error
                 D   E

54. Readers of the magazine were surprised that they had
            A   B

    not included any articles on urban sprawl or on public
                              C

    transportation and alternate routes into the city.
                       D

    No error
    E

55. After the accident left her with diminished mobility
    A   B

    and impaired vision, Genevieve found climbing up
                                   C

    and ascending the stairs increasingly difficult. No error
    D   E

56. Given his extensive background about medical
    A   B

    research, it was not surprising that Colin should have
                                              C

    been chosen to represent his department at the
                                            D

    institute's annual conference. No error
                                   E

GO ON TO THE NEXT PAGE ➡

57. There is now no doubt in <u>anyone's</u> mind that no one
A

deserved the grant more than <u>he;</u> <u>had</u> his colleagues
B C

not slighted his research at the time, he <u>might have</u>
D

acknowledged them in his acceptance speech. <u>No error</u>
E

58. <u>After eating</u> all the candy in the house, the greedy
A

children told <u>their</u> mother that <u>they</u> wanted to drink
B   C

<u>a cup</u> of hot chocolate. <u>No error</u>
D   E

59. It <u>would be</u> many years <u>before</u> the athlete's record, her
A   B

most <u>incredulous</u> feat in nearly a decade <u>of</u>
C   D

competition, would be broken by a foreign competitor.

<u>No error</u>
E

60. Ashley and Daphne asked <u>their</u> neighbor if he <u>had seen</u>
A   B

<u>whom</u> had stolen their picnic basket, but he
C

<u>hadn't noticed any</u> suspicious activity at the time the
D

basket was left unattended. <u>No error</u>
E

S T O P

IF YOU FINISH BEFORE TIME IS CALLED, YOU MAY CHECK YOUR WORK ON THIS TEST ONLY.
DO NOT TURN TO ANY OTHER TEST IN THIS BOOK.

SAT II Writing
Practice Test 3
Explanations

Calculating Your Score

Question Number	Correct Answer	Right	Wrong	Question Number	Correct Answer	Right	Wrong
1.	A	___	___	31.	C	___	___
2.	A	___	___	32.	A	___	___
3.	D	___	___	33.	A	___	___
4.	E	___	___	34.	B	___	___
5.	C	___	___	35.	C	___	___
6.	D	___	___	36.	B	___	___
7.	D	___	___	37.	E	___	___
8.	D	___	___	38.	E	___	___
9.	C	___	___	39.	A	___	___
10.	E	___	___	40.	D	___	___
11.	C	___	___	41.	B	___	___
12.	E	___	___	42.	C	___	___
13.	C	___	___	43.	C	___	___
14.	B	___	___	44.	B	___	___
15.	E	___	___	45.	C	___	___
16.	E	___	___	46.	B	___	___
17.	C	___	___	47.	D	___	___
18.	A	___	___	48.	A	___	___
19.	D	___	___	49.	D	___	___
20.	A	___	___	50.	B	___	___
21.	D	___	___	51.	B	___	___
22.	A	___	___	52.	A	___	___
23.	D	___	___	53.	B	___	___
24.	E	___	___	54.	B	___	___
25.	C	___	___	55.	D	___	___
26.	C	___	___	56.	B	___	___
27.	E	___	___	57.	E	___	___
28.	A	___	___	58.	D	___	___
29.	D	___	___	59.	C	___	___
30.	E	___	___	60.	C	___	___

Your raw score for the SAT II Writing test is a composite of your raw score in the multiple-choice section and your score on the essay. Once you have determined your composite score, use the conversion table on pages 16-17 to calculate your scaled score. To calculate your raw score, count the number of questions you answered correctly on the multiple choice: _____
$$\text{A}$$

Count the number of questions you answered incorrectly, and multiply that number by $\frac{1}{4}$:

$$\underset{\text{B}}{\rule{2cm}{0.4pt}} \times \frac{1}{4} = \underset{\text{C}}{\rule{2cm}{0.4pt}}$$

Subtract the value in field C from value in field A: $\underset{\text{D}}{\rule{2cm}{0.4pt}}$

Round the number to the nearest whole number: $\underset{\text{E}}{\rule{2cm}{0.4pt}}$

Take your score for the essay (ask a teacher to grade your essay or grade yourself) and multiply it by 3.43:

$$\underset{\text{F}}{\rule{2cm}{0.4pt}} \times 3.43 = \underset{\text{G}}{\rule{2cm}{0.4pt}}$$

Add the number in field E to the number in Field G: $\underset{\text{H}}{\rule{2cm}{0.4pt}}$

Round the number in field H. This is your SAT II Writing score: _____

Student Essays

Total Score: 10 (each reader gave the essay a 5)

Although adversity is associated with suffering and misery, it has a positive side as well: people, political movements, and countries can all become stronger through adversity because it often creates qualities such as perseverance and courage. Our country's independence from Britain is an example of this concept of strength from adversity, as is the work of groundbreaking scientists who were unwilling to sacrifice their beliefs to please other people.

In the 1700s George Grenville, representing the British government, imposed a series of taxes, including the Sugar and Stamp Acts, on the thirteen American colonies. Reacting to the infringment upon its previous independence, the colonial leaders fought to preserve their right to "no taxation without representation." This was not an easy position to take and the suffering that followed, for example the Boston Massacre and the battle of Long Island, cost the new country a great deal. Blood was shed and many lives lost. This did not stop Jefferson and his associates from writing the Declaration of Independence in 1776 and, after years of fighting and bloodshed, the country was independent and strengthened by its brush with adversity.

Galileo also displayed the ability to persist and triumph in the face of adversity. An Italian physicist who helped in the formation of scientific theories that modern science bases itself on nowadays, Galileo supported the argument that the Earth moves around the Sun. Not only was Galileo forced to suffer adversity when the Catholic Church excommunicated him for his beliefs, but also made to appear before the Inquisition and retract his own scientific discoveries. He was then punished with house arrest. And yet, Galileo's work with one of the first telescopes, with which he discovered the phases of Venus and Jupiter's major satellites, lives on. He chose to oppose the pope, which is why I think it is fair to look at his work as a triumph, a choice to defy the opinions of his time in the belief that he would eventually be recognized as great and humanity would benefit from his adversity.

Obviously, not all suffering is good. This is clear when we look at personal tragedy and at the individual lives lost in the Revolutionary War and in such scientists as Galileo. But if it is possible to persist and to learn from suffering beyond our control such as being orphaned or impoverished, we can emerge stronger.

Discussion:

The content and organization of this essay are impressive, but awkward phrasing and grammatical errors prevent it from achieving a perfect score.

The introduction, although short, effectively conveys the essay's argument and structure. The first sentence lays out the argument that adversity can result in strength, and the second sentence mentions the supporting evidence the writer uses in the two main body paragraphs.

In the second paragraph, the writer describes the Revolutionary War (although it's not mentioned by name until the final paragraph) as an example of a country gaining strength through adversity. The details the writer includes (such as dates, names of acts, specific people and events, and even a quotation) really enhance the essay.

The writer makes a few errors in this paragraph. *Infringement upon its previous independence* has a pronoun agreement error: the singular pronoun *its* doesn't agree with the plural noun phrase that follows, *colonial leaders*. The writer also uses *this*, an ambiguous pronoun, to begin two sentences. She could fix this error by rephrasing the sentences to start *This position* and *This bloodshed*, for example.

The third paragraph discusses the effects of adversity on Galileo. The writer could improve the paragraph by discussing how Galileo's belief that the Earth revolves around the Sun contributed to the Catholic Church's decision to excommunicate him. As it is now, the paragraph jumps from one idea to the other without explaining how the two are connected.

The phrasing of the sentences in the this paragraph is awkward. *An Italian physicist who helped in the formation of scientific theories that modern science bases itself on nowadays* is a clumsy clause, and it's not even necessary because the writer discusses Galileo's influence on modern science at the end of the paragraph. The writer's use of *I* near the end of the paragraph seems out of place in the otherwise formal essay. There are also several grammar and diction errors in this paragraph. The writer uses the construction *not only ... but also* incorrectly by not maintaining parallelism between the two clauses. The sentence should say *not only was Galileo forced ... but he was also punished* or *Galileo was not only forced ... but also punished*. The writer also makes a subject-verb agreement error (*Galileo's work ... live on*); to correct this error, the writer needs to change the plural verb *live* to the singular *lives*.

The conclusion is the weakest part of this essay. Most readers will understand what the writer means by *the individual lives lost in the Revolutionary War and in such scientists as Galileo*, but the phrase itself makes little sense. For the most part, the conclusion merely rehashes what the writer said in the essay instead of providing a real concluding thought.

Total Score: 6 (each reader gave the essay a 3)

Adversity makes everybody stronger, no two ways about it. If you don't know what it is to deal with adversity, one can't learn from your mistakes or know how to appreciate anything. For example, my grandfather grew up in very poor circumstances, sometimes without a house or food. Because of that, he was able to work hard and appreciate everything he can provide for my sister and I.

Not all people thrive on adversity but then they are weak to begin with and don't know what it is to put yourself through college and not count on financial aid from your parents. I am lucky because I don't face that kind of adversity in my life and have items others take for granted. Even basic amenities, running water, warm cloathes. Not everybody can pay for a TV, and then they all think they deserve DVDs because they don't have anyone in his or her families who really expereinced adversity firsthand.

Also, if you look to history like the first people who came to this country and also the slaves, you can see how a people can grow stronger because they had hard lives. In the case of Irish who came here because of the potato famin, and slaves who were taken against their will, they learned and became successful because they were so motivated to raise themselves from bad circumstances. Concluding, there is nothing great for those who are suffering but they can teach others by setting strong examples of working hard. This country teaches us to believe in the American Dream and if people hadn't suffered so we could be who we are and do what we want and have all the DVDs and free speech newspapers, then the fourfathers would have acheived nothing.

Discussion:

This writer rambles and makes multiple grammar errors, but the essay is saved from getting a lower score by its use of potentially sophisticated evidence.

One of the major problems of the essay is its lack of organization. Although the first paragraph presents an argument (*adversity makes everybody stronger*), the paragraph doesn't work as an introduction because it doesn't introduce the evidence used in the essay; instead, the writer discusses the example of the grandfather. The second paragraph discusses the writer's appreciation for what she has and mentions people who don't appreciate the luxuries they possess because they have never faced economic adversity.

In the third (and last) paragraph, the writer moves to an entirely different subject: people who came to the United States to escape adversity and slaves who were brought against their will (unfortunately, the writer fails to distinguish between the experiences of the two groups). This paragraph also includes the writer's concluding thoughts.

The writer could improve the organization of the essay by including an introduction that clearly states the argument and mentions the three pieces of supporting evidence: the grandfather's experience, the writer's own experience, and the immigrants' and slaves' experiences. Each piece of evidence should be discussed in its own main body paragraph, and the essay should end with a separate conclusion.

The essay's language is another problem. The writer has an unsophisticated style (*no two ways about it*) made worse by grammar and spelling errors. *If you don't know what it is to suffer adversity, one can't learn from your mistakes*, for example, makes the pronoun agreement error of switching between *you* and *one*. *Between my sister and I* also has a pronoun error; *I* should be replaced by *me* because a preposition such as *between* needs to be followed by the objective case (*me, him, us, them*, for example). The writer misspells *clothes* as *cloathes*, *experienced* as *expereinced*, *famine* as *famin*, *achieved* as *acheived*, and *forefathers* as *fourfathers*.

The strongest aspect of this essay is its content. The references to the Irish potato famine and the slave trade show that the writer has some ability to consider historical events in light of an essay topic, but the writer fails to develop these references into concrete support for her argument. The writer's discussion of people who don't appreciate their possessions should probably be cut down or cut out, particularly the sentences that say *those who are weak to begin with* and *they all think they deserve DVDs*. On the SAT II Writing, you should try to avoid criticizing others because you don't want to offend your examiners.

Also, unless personal anecdotes are specifically called for by the question, they tend not to work as well as references to literature, history, or current events. In this essay, however, the anecdote about the grandfather works because it is relevant to the essay question. The writer could make the example stronger by providing specific details of the grandfather's experience and demonstrating the link between the adversity the grandfather faced and the gains he made because of it.

Identifying Sentence Errors

1. **(A)** *Subject-Verb Agreement*

Subject-verb agreement in *neither/nor* constructions can be tricky. In this sentence, you have one plural subject, *parents*, and one singular subject, *sister*. The subject that's closer to the verb (in other words, the subject that follows *nor*) determines whether the verb is singular or plural. Since the singular noun *sister* follows *nor*, you need to use the singular verb *is* in this sentence. If you picked (D) because *regardless* sounds wrong, remember that *regardless* is a word, but *irregardless* is not.

2. **(A)** *Pronoun Shift*

This sentence contains a pronoun agreement error because the pronoun switches from *you* to *one*. Although both *you* and *one* are underlined, you should change *you* because it occurs only once in the sentence, while *one* shows up twice (*one* and *oneself*).

3. **(D)** *Faulty Comparison*

This sentence wants to say that Asia's size is significantly larger than Europe's size. Instead, it says that Asia's size is larger than Europe. In order to fix this faulty comparison, you need to change *Europe* to *Europe's* or *Europe's size*.

You may not have liked the sound of *sheer*, but it's being used correctly to emphasize the greatness of Asia's size.

4.   (E)   *No Error*

No error.

5.   (C)   *Parallelism*

Whenever you see a list, you should be on the lookout for parallelism errors. *Extended hours* and *microfilm services* are both noun phrases, so the third item in the list also needs to be a noun. *Helping new cardholders navigating the stacks*, though, is a verb phrase. In order to correct the faulty parallelism, you need to change the verb phrase into a noun phrase: *help for new cardholders navigating the stacks*.

6.   (D)   *Adverb*

In this sentence, the sitcom is compared to every other sitcom of its kind. When you have a comparison involving more than two things, you need to use a superlative modifier like *dumbest* rather than a comparitive modifier like *dumber*. Superlatives usually end in *–est*, and comparitives usually end in *–er*.

7.   (D)   *Wrong Word*

Urbane is the wrong word in this sentence because it means suave and sophisticated. *Urban* means a characteristic of a city, and it's the right word in this context.

8.   (D)   *Pronoun Agreement*

Whenever you see a singular pronoun such as *each, everybody, nobody, somebody,* or *something*, you should watch out for a pronoun agreement error. In this sentence, the singular noun phrase *each student* is modified by the plural pronoun *their*. In order to have pronoun agreement, *their* needs to be replaced by *his, her,* or *his or her*.

9.   (C)   *Subject-Verb Agreement*

The subject of this sentence is the singular noun *persistence*, so the verb that follows it must be the singular *is* instead of the plural *are*. Subject-verb agreement in this sentence is tricky because the sentence appears to have two subjects—*persistence* and *skill*—but, because *skill* appears after the prepositional phrase *in addition to*, it's not part of the subject.

10.   (E)   *No Error*

No error.

11.   (C)   *Pronoun*

Who is *they*? The pronoun is ambiguous because it doesn't refer to anyone or anything mentioned in the sentence. The pronoun *it*, on the other hand, is not ambiguous because the sentence eventually shows that *it* refers to *the ground*.

12.   (E)   *No Error*

No error.

13.   (C)   *Adverb*

Carefully is an adverb incorrectly modifying the noun *study*. Adjectives, not adverbs, modify nouns. In order to correct this sentence, you need to replace *carefully* with the adjective *careful*.

14. **(B)**   *Fragment*

The sentence in the question is a fragment because it lacks a subject and verb. You can create a real sentence by changing *that speak* to *speak*, making an independent clause: *people speak*.

15. **(E)**   *No Error*

No error.

16. **(E)**   *No Error*

No error.

17. **(C)**   *Parallelism*

According to the rules of parallelism, the gerund *constraining* needs to be followed by another gerund—not by the infinitive *to hinder*. If the wetsuits cling *without constraining*, they must also cling *without hindering*.

18. **(A)**   *Wrong Word*

Dissemble and *disassemble* mean two different things. *To dissemble* means to lie, and *to disassemble* means to take apart. The agents in this sentence are taking apart a table; therefore, you should use *disassemble* instead of *dissemble*.

19. **(D)**   *Idiom*

The correct expression is *paid a visit to the Godiva shop*, not *paid a visit at the Godiva shop*. The gerund *hoping* may sound wrong to you, but *hoping* is used correctly in an adverbial clause that describes why the girls went to the shop.

20. **(A)**   *Tense*

The girl bases her decision to attend a rural college on her childhood spent in a large city. The decision she makes in the present depends on something that happened in the past. If you want to show the order of events in this sentence, you need to change *being* (present tense) to *having been* (past tense), making clear that she was raised in the city before she chose to attend a rural college.

Improving Sentence Errors

21. **(D)**   *Tense*

The original sentence has a verb tense error. *Will be found* (future tense) doesn't make sense because the sentence wants to describe what happened in the past—between the discovery of plutonium in 1940 and the present time. Trace amounts of plutonium were found in nature in the past, so *will be found* needs to be changed to the past tense: *since then it has been found in trace amounts in nature*.

22. **(A)**   *No Error*

No error.

23. (D)   *Passive Voice*

The use of the passive voice makes this sentence sound clumsy. You can fix this problem by stating right off the bat that *the new chef has made significant changes to the menu*. Choice (E), which also uses the active voice, incorrectly changes the verb to the present tense (*makes*). The sentence should say that the chef has made changes in the past, not that he's making changes right now.

24. (E)   *Misplaced Modifier*

Improving Sentence questions often play host to misplaced modifiers. The original sentence implies that the balance of world trade is competing with newly industrialized countries, but what the sentence wants to say is that economically established countries are competing with newly industrialized ones. In order to fix this problem, you need to move the modifier (*competing with newly industrialized countries...*) next to the noun phrase it modifies (*economically established countries*). Both (D) and (E) make this change, but the phrasing of (D) makes the sentence confusing, so (E) is the correct answer.

25. (C)   *Parallelism*

The original sentence has a parallelism error. The gerund *endangering* is followed by the the phrase *we do destroy species*. In order to fix the error, you need to rewrite *we do destroy species* as a gerund. (C) makes this correction: *we have been endangering and destroying species*.

26. (C)   *Fragment*

The original sentence is actually a sentence fragment, lacking an independent clause. In order to make the sentence complete, you need to change the form of *playing*, which doesn't function as a verb in this sentence. Choice (C) correctly changes the verb to *played*, which makes the sentence complete (*Peter played*) and indicates that Peter's playing occurred in the past.

27. (E)   *Parallelism*

The original sentence breaks the parallelism rule. If you think of the verb *to be* as an equal sign, then in this sentence you have a gerund (*confining*) incorrectly equal to an infinitive (*to keep*). You need to change the infinitive *to keep* into the gerund *keeping*. While (C), (D), and (E) all make this change, (C) and (D) use the idiomatically-incorrect phrase *controversial source*, which suggests that a source itself is controversial. *Source of controversy*, on the other hand, means that something (for example, keeping animals in zoos) produces controversy. (E) is the correct answer.

28. (A)   *No Error*

No error.

29. (D)   *Pronoun Agreement*

Woodrow Wilson's plan is a singular entity, but *they*, the pronoun that modifies the plan, is plural. Both (D) and (E) correct the error, substituting *it* for *they*. (E) makes a tense error: the sentence begins in the past tense (*was crucial*), and (E) illogically shifts to the present tense (*faces*).

30. (E)   *Pronoun Case*

You need to figure out whether to use *who* or *whom* in this sentence. *Who* performs an action; it has the same function as pronouns such as *I, she, we,* and *they. Whom* receives an action; it has the same function as *me, her, us,* and *them.* The owners want to address their complaint *to* something. A preposition, such as *to*, needs to be followed by *whom*, a pronoun that receives an action. If you're having trouble figuring out which pronoun to use, try substituting *I* for *who* and *me* for *whom* in the sentence: *to I* sounds wrong, but *to me* sounds right.

31. **(C)**   *Pronoun*

The object of the preposition *of* is the gerund *having*, not the pronoun *him*. The purpose of *him* is to show who does or "owns" the *having*, so you need to change *him* to the possessive pronoun *his*. Both (C) and (E) make this change, but (E) incorrectly uses the present tense (*in case she forgets it*). Since the action of the sentence occurs in the past, the act of forgetting must occur in the past too.

32. **(A)**   *No Error*

No error.

33. **(A)**   *No Error*

No error.

34. **(B)**   *Run-on*

The original sentence is a run-on because two independent clauses are joined incorrectly by a mere comma. A comma is too weak to join independent clauses without the addition of a conjunction (such as *and* or *yet*), but a semicolon is strong enough to do the trick. Choice (B) correctly links the two clauses with a semicolon. Although choice (D) also uses a semicolon, the phrase following the semicolon is a dependent clause (meaning that it can't stand on its own), and semicolons should be used to join independent clauses only.

35. **(C)**   *Idiom*

The correct idiom is *as famous for this as for that*. (C) is the only answer that uses the idiom correctly.

36. **(B)**   *Run-on*

This sentence uses a comma to join two clauses that could be complete sentences on their own, but a comma isn't enough punctuation to hold the clauses together. You need to figure out how to join the clauses in a grammatically correct way. You can rule out (C) and (E) immediately because they both turn the sentence into a fragment with no independent clause. Notice that (B) and (D) try to fix the problem by making one of the clauses dependent on the other, but (D) has a tense error, since it follows the verb *fascinated* (past tense) with the verb *seeks* (present tense).

37. **(E)**   *Passive Voice*

If a sentence seems to take a while to make its point, you may have a passive voice problem on your hands. The passive voice is usually easy to correct. In this case, you can switch the order of *the tree* and *Alex* and get rid of *was*: *When Alex chopped down the tree*. Choice (E) is correct.

38. **(E)**   *Subject-Verb Agreement*

The subject of this sentence is *verbal dexterity*, a singular noun phrase. *Reading and writing* are added in a prepositional phrase (*in addition to*), so they don't count as part of the subject. Because the subject is singular, you need the singular verb *is* instead of the plural *are*. Both (D) and (E) use the singular verb, but (D) is incorrect because it makes the idiomatic error, *quality on an editor*. The correct expression is *quality of an editor*.

Improving Paragraphs

39. **(A)** *Revision*

The original sentence tries to say that there are many reasons why people travel. Choice (A) is the clearest revision of this sentence: *people travel for a variety of reasons*. Although choices (B) and (D) get the right idea across, they're wordy, and they contain errors: (B) incorrectly uses *of course*, and (D) has an agreement error with its singular subject and plural verb. Choices (C) and (E) distort the meaning of the sentence: (C) suggests that *people vary*, and (E) suggests that *travel varies*.

40. **(D)** *Revision*

Farthering is not a word, so you can rule out choices (A) and (B). *Facilitating*, which means bringing about, is a word, and it works in the context of the sentence. Choice (C) has an idiom error: *in* should not follow *communication*. Choice (D), which is the correct answer, fixes this error: *communication between*. Choice (E) is wrong because *fabricating*, which means making up (as in make believe), doesn't make sense in this sentence.

41. **(B)** *Revision*

A sentence that uses the phrase *being as* will almost always be wrong on the SAT II Writing. The original sentence and choice (C) both use this phrase, so you can rule them out for now. Choice (E) is definitely wrong, since it's a sentence fragment, lacking a subject and verb. Choice (D) doesn't say that the mother was pregnant with the author at the time of the author's first trip, leaving the meaning of the sentence ambiguous. Choice (B) is the correct answer because it states all the information from the original sentence in a clear, grammatically correct way.

42. **(C)** *Analysis*

In sentence 11, the author contrasts comfortable living conditions in America (living rooms and books) with poor living conditions in other countries (lack of real houses), so choice (C) is correct. If you weren't sure what *disparity* means, you still might have been able to get the right answer by eliminating the other choices.

43. **(C)** *Combining Sentences*

You want to combine sentences 13 and 14 in a logical, grammatically correct way. Choice (A), although grammatically correct, is an illogical combination of the sentences. *Despite* suggests that the sentences are incompatible with each other and that they contrast in some way. Choice (B) is also an illogical combination; it says that international travel is affordable *because* people are traveling for pleasure. Choices (D) and (E) both contain grammatical errors: (D) is a run-on sentence, and (E) has an agreement error with its plural subject and singular verb. Choice (C), the correct answer, combines the two sentences logically without making any grammatical errors.

44. (B)   *Analysis*

The author of this essay frequently refers to her childhood experiences and to her parents' opinions, making the piece anecdotal in nature. If you don't know what *anecdotal* means, you can narrow down the answer choices by ruling out obviously wrong ones. The slangy prose and personal stories make the essay the opposite of formal, so you know choice (A) is wrong. The author never contrasts her argument, which is that people travel for a variety of reasons, with a counterargument, which could be that people travel for one reason, so you can rule out choice (C). Choice (E) is wrong because the author doesn't cite any data. The proof for her argument comes primarily from personal experience.

45. (C)   *Analysis*

The two sentences given by choice (C) are the least essential part of the essay. They talk about unscrupulous sellers of organic products and the government's attempts to stop these sellers. These sentences digress from the main topic of the essay, and their subject is never mentioned again.

46. (B)   *Revision*

Choice (B) is the best revision, conveying the meaning of the original sentence in a grammatically-correct way. Choice (A) is wrong because it uses the pronoun *this* ambiguously. Choice (C) incorrectly suggests that *government controls*, rather than the effect of the controls, will not be immediate. Choice (D) is wordy, and choice (E) doesn't say anything about the government.

47. (D)   *Revision*

Sentence 10 is a run-on. Choice (D) is the best revision of the sentence because it logically relates the three ideas in the original sentence: the high cost of organic produce, the reason for this high cost, and an alternative to organic products. Choices (A) and (C) fail to relate these ideas clearly and logically. Choices (B) and (E) are wordy and unclear.

48. (A)   *Analysis*

In sentence 13, the author tells the reader to consider the country of origin of a food product before buying it; in other words, the author instructs the reader to do something, so choice (A) is correct.

49. (D)   *Analysis*

When a question capitalizes EXCEPT, you should take notice. In this case, you're looking for what the author doesn't do in the essay. Choice (D) is the correct answer because the author never mentions any environmentalists.

50. (B)   *Revision*

The easiest way to answer this question is to try out each of the answer choices and see which answer choice sounds right. Ending the sentence after the word *bacteria* keeps the sentence concise without eliminating any important information. If you stop reading the sentence after *bacteria*, you should realize that the last phrase, *that can be transported on melon and even transferred into your fruit when you slice it open*, is unnecessary. None of the other answer choices makes as much sense as (B).

Test 3 Explanations

Identifying Sentence Errors

51. **(B)**   *Subject-Verb Agreement*

Whenever you see a subject and a verb separated by a long prepositional phrase or dependent clause, you should check for a subject-verb agreement error. The subject of this sentence is the singular noun *crowd*. *Were*, the verb that follows it, is plural and needs to be replaced by the singular verb *was*.

Another way to check for incorrect pronouns is to complete the comparison. *She was taller than him* is an incomplete version of *she was taller than him was*. *Him*, in this completed sentence, sounds wrong. *She was taller than he was* sounds right, so you know the correct pronoun is *he*.

52. **(A)**   *Pronoun*

In this sentence, the subject, *travelers*, is plural, so you need to modify it with a plural pronoun, *their*. The pronoun *their* in choice (D) is correct because it modifies the plural noun phrase *holiday resorts*.

53. **(B)**   *Double Negative*

When you put two words with negative meanings side by side, they cancel each other out. *She would have hardly no time* actually means that she would have time. One of the negative words needs to go; you can say instead: *she would have no time* or *she would have hardly any time*.

54. **(B)**   *Pronoun*

This sentence is a little bit tricky because the ambiguous pronoun (*they*) is hard to spot. You may assume that the plural pronoun *they* refers to the plural noun *readers*, but if you read the sentence carefully, you'll realize that the readers probably weren't the ones responsible for including articles in the magazine. *They* probably refers to the magazine's editors, but you can't be sure, since the pronoun is ambiguous.

55. **(D)**   *Redundancy*

This sentence says the same thing twice. *Climbing up* and *ascending* have the same meaning. You need only one of them to get your point across. In order to get rid of the redundancy, remove *and ascending* from the sentence.

56. **(B)**   *Idiom*

This sentence contains an idiom error. You should say that someone has a background *in* medical research, not a background *about* medical research.

57. **(E)**   *No Error*

No error.

58. **(D)**   *Number Agreement*

Number agreement errors are really hard to catch with your ear because they're made frequently in speech. Each child (singular) wants to drink a cup (singular) of hot chocolate, so the greedy children (plural) want to drink *cups* (plural) of hot chocolate. In order to fix the number agreement error, you need to change the singular noun *a cup* to the plural noun *cups*.

59. **(C)**   *Wrong Word*

The athlete's feat was *incredible*, not *incredulous*. *Incredible* means defying credibility or believability. *Incredulous* means unbelieving and almost always applies to people, not to things like athlete's feats.

60. **(C)**   *Pronoun*

Who performs an action, and *whom* receives it. You need to replace *whom* with a pronoun capable of taking the picnic basket—in other words, a pronoun that performs an action—so *who* is the right word.

SAT II Writing Test 4

WRITING TEST 4 ANSWER SHEET

1. Ⓐ Ⓑ Ⓒ Ⓓ Ⓔ	21. Ⓐ Ⓑ Ⓒ Ⓓ Ⓔ	41. Ⓐ Ⓑ Ⓒ Ⓓ Ⓔ
2. Ⓐ Ⓑ Ⓒ Ⓓ Ⓔ	22. Ⓐ Ⓑ Ⓒ Ⓓ Ⓔ	42. Ⓐ Ⓑ Ⓒ Ⓓ Ⓔ
3. Ⓐ Ⓑ Ⓒ Ⓓ Ⓔ	23. Ⓐ Ⓑ Ⓒ Ⓓ Ⓔ	43. Ⓐ Ⓑ Ⓒ Ⓓ Ⓔ
4. Ⓐ Ⓑ Ⓒ Ⓓ Ⓔ	24. Ⓐ Ⓑ Ⓒ Ⓓ Ⓔ	44. Ⓐ Ⓑ Ⓒ Ⓓ Ⓔ
5. Ⓐ Ⓑ Ⓒ Ⓓ Ⓔ	25. Ⓐ Ⓑ Ⓒ Ⓓ Ⓔ	45. Ⓐ Ⓑ Ⓒ Ⓓ Ⓔ
6. Ⓐ Ⓑ Ⓒ Ⓓ Ⓔ	26. Ⓐ Ⓑ Ⓒ Ⓓ Ⓔ	46. Ⓐ Ⓑ Ⓒ Ⓓ Ⓔ
7. Ⓐ Ⓑ Ⓒ Ⓓ Ⓔ	27. Ⓐ Ⓑ Ⓒ Ⓓ Ⓔ	47. Ⓐ Ⓑ Ⓒ Ⓓ Ⓔ
8. Ⓐ Ⓑ Ⓒ Ⓓ Ⓔ	28. Ⓐ Ⓑ Ⓒ Ⓓ Ⓔ	48. Ⓐ Ⓑ Ⓒ Ⓓ Ⓔ
9. Ⓐ Ⓑ Ⓒ Ⓓ Ⓔ	29. Ⓐ Ⓑ Ⓒ Ⓓ Ⓔ	49. Ⓐ Ⓑ Ⓒ Ⓓ Ⓔ
10. Ⓐ Ⓑ Ⓒ Ⓓ Ⓔ	30. Ⓐ Ⓑ Ⓒ Ⓓ Ⓔ	50. Ⓐ Ⓑ Ⓒ Ⓓ Ⓔ
11. Ⓐ Ⓑ Ⓒ Ⓓ Ⓔ	31. Ⓐ Ⓑ Ⓒ Ⓓ Ⓔ	51. Ⓐ Ⓑ Ⓒ Ⓓ Ⓔ
12. Ⓐ Ⓑ Ⓒ Ⓓ Ⓔ	32. Ⓐ Ⓑ Ⓒ Ⓓ Ⓔ	52. Ⓐ Ⓑ Ⓒ Ⓓ Ⓔ
13. Ⓐ Ⓑ Ⓒ Ⓓ Ⓔ	33. Ⓐ Ⓑ Ⓒ Ⓓ Ⓔ	53. Ⓐ Ⓑ Ⓒ Ⓓ Ⓔ
14. Ⓐ Ⓑ Ⓒ Ⓓ Ⓔ	34. Ⓐ Ⓑ Ⓒ Ⓓ Ⓔ	54. Ⓐ Ⓑ Ⓒ Ⓓ Ⓔ
15. Ⓐ Ⓑ Ⓒ Ⓓ Ⓔ	35. Ⓐ Ⓑ Ⓒ Ⓓ Ⓔ	55. Ⓐ Ⓑ Ⓒ Ⓓ Ⓔ
16. Ⓐ Ⓑ Ⓒ Ⓓ Ⓔ	36. Ⓐ Ⓑ Ⓒ Ⓓ Ⓔ	56. Ⓐ Ⓑ Ⓒ Ⓓ Ⓔ
17. Ⓐ Ⓑ Ⓒ Ⓓ Ⓔ	37. Ⓐ Ⓑ Ⓒ Ⓓ Ⓔ	57. Ⓐ Ⓑ Ⓒ Ⓓ Ⓔ
18. Ⓐ Ⓑ Ⓒ Ⓓ Ⓔ	38. Ⓐ Ⓑ Ⓒ Ⓓ Ⓔ	58. Ⓐ Ⓑ Ⓒ Ⓓ Ⓔ
19. Ⓐ Ⓑ Ⓒ Ⓓ Ⓔ	39. Ⓐ Ⓑ Ⓒ Ⓓ Ⓔ	59. Ⓐ Ⓑ Ⓒ Ⓓ Ⓔ
20. Ⓐ Ⓑ Ⓒ Ⓓ Ⓔ	40. Ⓐ Ⓑ Ⓒ Ⓓ Ⓔ	60. Ⓐ Ⓑ Ⓒ Ⓓ Ⓔ

WRITING TEST 4

Part A

Time — 20 minutes

You have twenty minutes to plan and write an essay on the topic assigned below. DO NOT WRITE ON ANOTHER TOPIC. AN ESSAY ON ANOTHER TOPIC IS NOT ACCEPTABLE.

The essay is assigned to give you an opportunity to show how well you can write. You should, therefore, take care to express your thoughts on the topic clearly and effectively. How well you write is much more important than how much you write, but to cover the topic adequately you will probably need to write more than one paragraph. Be specific.

Your essay must be written on the following two pages. You will find that you have enough space if you write on every line, avoid wide margins, and keep your handwriting to a reasonable size. It is important to remember that what you write will be read by someone who is not familiar with your handwriting. Try to write or print so that what you are writing is legible to the reader.

Consider the following statement and assignment. Then write the essay as directed.

"Necessity is the mother of invention."

Assignment: Choose one example from personal experience, current events, or history, literature, or any other discipline and use this example to write an essay in which you agree or disagree with the statement above. Your essay should be specific.

DO NOT WRITE YOUR ESSAY IN YOUR TEST BOOK. You will receive credit only for what you write on your answer sheet.

WHEN YOUR SUPERVISOR ANNOUNCES THAT TWENTY MINUTES HAVE PASSED, YOU MUST STOP WRITING THE ESSAY AND GO ON TO PART B IF YOU HAVE NOT ALREADY DONE SO. IF YOU FINISH YOUR ESSAY BEFORE THIS ANNOUNCEMENT, GO ON TO PART B AT ONCE.

BEGIN WRITING YOUR ESSAY ON THE ANSWER SHEET.

WRITING TEST

Part A

Time — 20 minutes

_____
_____
_____
_____
_____
_____
_____
_____
_____
_____
_____
_____
_____
_____
_____
_____
_____
_____
_____
_____
_____
_____
_____
_____
_____

WRITING TEST

Part A

Time — 20 minutes

WRITING TEST

Part B

Time — 40 minutes

Directions: The following sentences test your knowledge of grammar, usage, diction (choice of words), and idiom.

Some sentences are correct.
No sentence contains more than one error.

You will find that the error, if there is one, is underlined and lettered. Elements of the sentence that are not underlined will not be changed. In choosing answers, follow the requirements of standard written English.

If there is an error, select the one underlined part that must be changed to make the sentence correct and fill in the corresponding oval on your answer sheet.

If there is no answer, fill in answer oval Ⓔ.

EXAMPLE:

The other delegates and him immediately
    A   B   C

accepted the resolution drafted by the
                              D

neutral states. No error
                    E

SAMPLE ANSWER:

Ⓐ ● Ⓒ Ⓓ Ⓔ

1. In addition to snowboarding, fencing, and swimming,
                                            A

   the Olympic athlete listed creative writing among her
                        B   C

   hobbies as well. No error
          D   E

2. Many jazz legends who traveled abroad have
                     A   B

   commented on the enthusiasm of foreign audiences for
              C   D

   American music. No error
                   E

3. The percentage of teenagers who smoke have
                                          A

   continued to increase despite numerous advertising
            B   C

   campaigns highlighting the dangers of tobacco.
             D

   No error
   E

4. To prevent littering, the parks commission distributed
   A

   garbage cans around the perimeters of their
                   B   C

   conservatory's gardens. No error
   D   E

5. The visiting ambassador's speech was interrupted far
                                                    A

   more frequently than either his security detail nor the
                      B   C

   local police had anticipated. No error
                   D   E

GO ON TO THE NEXT PAGE ➡

6. When <u>applying for</u> an internship program, you must,
         A

   <u>regardless</u> of your qualifications, present yourself <u>as</u>
   B   C

   <u>confidently</u> as possible at your interview. <u>No error</u>
   D   E

7. <u>Curled in</u> the window seat <u>of</u> the cottage's living room
   A   B

   <u>was</u> the owner's tabby cat and three <u>nursing</u> kittens.
   C   D

   <u>No error</u>
   E

8. Practically indistinguishable <u>from</u> her twin sister,
                     A

   Emily was accustomed to <u>be</u> mistaken <u>for</u> her <u>more</u>
                      B   C   D

   famous sibling. <u>No error</u>
                E

9. While <u>being</u> interviewed for a newspaper article, the
   A

   artist was dismayed <u>to</u> discover that his name
                  B

   <u>had been</u> mispelled on the posters for his <u>upcoming</u>
   C   D

   show. <u>No error</u>
        E

10. The psychiatrist appointed <u>by</u> the court <u>recommended</u>
                       A   B

   that the prisoner <u>be placed</u> in custody for an <u>indecisive</u>
                  C   D

   period of time. <u>No error</u>
               E

11. <u>In addition to</u> forcing her subjects into uncomfortable
   A

   poses, the portrait artist <u>was</u> notorious <u>for</u>
                     B   C

   complaining that her fees were not <u>hardly</u> as high as
                           D

   they should have been. <u>No error</u>
                     E

12. Many <u>commercially</u> successful writers complain that
          A

   <u>their</u> peers who deal <u>with</u> academic or literary
   B   C

   themes are held in higher esteem than <u>them</u>. <u>No error</u>
                             D   E

13. The store's decision to <u>rise</u> prices <u>will alienate</u>
                     A   B

   consumers and detract <u>from</u> the store's <u>profits</u>.
                      C   D

   <u>No error</u>
   E

14. <u>Working</u> deftly, the chef created a feast <u>using</u> <u>only</u>
   A   B   C

   the items that <u>were growing</u> in his garden. <u>No error</u>
                 D   E

15. <u>By far</u> the <u>weakest</u> member of the team, Paul was
   A   B

   determined to make up <u>in</u> personality what he lacked
                      C

   <u>through</u> skill. <u>No error</u>
   D   E

16. If he <u>had had</u> fun, the tourist <u>might not be changing</u>
        A   B

   his plans, <u>and</u> he would have stayed <u>until</u> the
             C   D

   scheduled end to the trip. <u>No error</u>
                     E

17. In a <u>series of</u> town meetings, the residents were
       A

   <u>informed</u> that construction of the Olympic stadium
   B

   would <u>effect</u> traffic patterns for <u>nearly</u> eight months.
        C   D

   <u>No error</u>
   E

GO ON TO THE NEXT PAGE

18. <u>Although</u> many people once <u>believed</u> that Tchaikovsky
    A   B

    died <u>from</u> cholera after drinking contaminated water,
         C

    <u>and</u> there is now a theory that he died by committing
     D

    suicide. <u>No error</u>
            E

19. If you <u>are</u> interested in <u>learning about</u> the early
       A   B

    printing presses, <u>one</u> should visit the current exhibit <u>at</u>
                 C   D

    the local museum. <u>No error</u>
                E

20. Pundits who observed the underdog's <u>grassroots</u>
                                      A

    campaign <u>were</u> quick <u>to</u> point out the effectiveness of
            B   C

    his aggressive approach over his <u>rival</u>. <u>No error</u>
                              D   E

GO ON TO THE NEXT PAGE

WRITING TEST

Directions: The following sentences test correctness and effectiveness of expression. In choosing answers, follow the requirements of standard written English; that is, pay attention to grammar, choice of words, sentence construction, and punctuation.

In each of the following sentences, part of the sentence or the entire sentence is underlined. Beneath each sentence you will find five ways of phrasing the underlined part. Choice A repeats the original; the other four are different.

Choose the answer that best expresses the meaning of the original sentence. If you think the original is better than any of the alternatives, choose it; otherwise choose one of the others. Your choice should produce the most effective sentence—clear and precise, without awkwardness or ambiguity.

EXAMPLE: SAMPLE ANSWER:

Laura Ingalls Wilder published her first book
and she was sixty-five years old then.

(A) and she was sixty-five years old then
(B) when she was sixty-five
(C) at age sixty-five years old
(D) upon the reaching of sixty-five years
(E) at the time when she was sixty-five

21. Ragtime music, characterized by a syncopated melodic line and regularly-accented accompaniment, is most often associated with the piano.

(A) Ragtime music, characterized by a syncopated melodic line and regularly accented accompaniment, is most often associated with the piano.
(B) Ragtime music, characterized by a syncopated melodic line and regularly accented accompaniment, are most often associated with the piano.
(C) Ragtime music is characterized by a syncopated melodic line and regularly accented accompaniment which is most often associated with the piano.
(D) Ragtime music is characterized by a syncopated melodic line and regularly accented accompaniment, which are most often associated with the piano.
(E) Characterized by a syncopated melodic line and regularly accented accompaniment, ragtime music most often associates with the piano.

22. The idea of a meritocracy, a government selected according to merit, is as appealing than it is difficult to implement.

(A) as appealing than it is difficult to implement
(B) as appealing and then it is difficult to implement
(C) as appealing as it can be difficult to implement
(D) as appealing as it is difficult to implement
(E) as appealing as they are difficult to implement

GO ON TO THE NEXT PAGE

23. While concealing the fact that she had drawn a spade, <u>the fact that the professional gambler was hiding a duplicate set of cards was what she inadvertently drew attention to</u>.

    (A) the fact that the professional gambler was hiding a duplicate set of cards was what she inadvertently drew attention to
    (B) the fact that the professional gambler had concealed a duplicate set of cards was what she inadvertently hid
    (C) the professional gambler drew inadvertent attention to the fact of a hidden set of duplicate cards
    (D) the professional gambler inadvertently drew attention to the duplicate set of cards she hides
    (E) the professional gambler inadvertently drew attention to the fact that she had hidden a duplicate set of cards

24. None of the king's <u>courtiers were willing to commit treason, regardless of</u> the money the rebels had offered.

    (A) courtiers were willing to commit treason, regardless of
    (B) courtiers were willing to commit treason, regardless to
    (C) courtiers was willing to commit treason, regardless of
    (D) courtiers was willing to commit treason, regardless to
    (E) courtiers who was willing to have committed treason, regardless of

25. In order to prevent any futher losses, <u>the company's board of directors quickly moving to cut costs</u>.

    (A) the company's board of directors quickly moving to cut costs
    (B) the company's board of directors quickly moved to cut costs
    (C) as a result the company's board of directors were quickly moving to cut costs
    (D) the company's board of directors were quickly to move to cut costs
    (E) yet the company's board of directors quickly moving to cut costs

26. This year the school decided to offer courses <u>on typing, word processing, and how to use the Internet</u>.

    (A) on typing, word processing, and how to use the Internet
    (B) on typing, word processing, and using the Internet
    (C) in which students learned typing, word processing, and how to use the Internet
    (D) in which students learned typing, word processing, and additionally to use the Internet
    (E) during which students were taught typing, word processing, and using the Internet

27. Before the development of modern astronomy, people believed that each of the seven moving stars they saw <u>was constantly changing its position in relation to Earth</u>.

    (A) was constantly changing its position in relation to Earth
    (B) were constantly changing its position relating to Earth
    (C) changed their position relative to Earth
    (D) were changing their position relative to that of the Earth
    (E) was constantly changing their positions relative to those of the Earth

28. <u>It was the governor's suggestion that his campaign manager take some time off, that way he could recharge his batteries.</u>

    (A) It was the governor's suggestion that his campaign manager take some time off, that way he could recharge his batteries.
    (B) It was the governor's suggestion that in order to recharge, specifically his batteries, his campaign manager take some time off.
    (C) The governor suggested that his campaign manager, in order to recharge his batteries, takes some time off.
    (D) The governor suggested that his campaign manager take some time off in order to recharge his batteries.
    (E) The governor's suggestion to his campaign manager was so that he take some time off in order to recharge his batteries.

GO ON TO THE NEXT PAGE ➤

29. Neither of the two doctors <u>are seeking work at the local hospital, choosing instead to focus on work</u> in the private sector.

    (A) are seeking work at the local hospital, choosing instead to focus on work

    (B) is seeking work at the local hospital, choosing instead to focus on work

    (C) is seeking work at the local hospital, choosing instead to focus on their work

    (D) is seeking work at the local hospital, having chosen instead to focus on their work

    (E) are seeking work at the local hospital, choosing instead to focus on their work

30. <u>Being not a writer himself, the champion golfer</u> decided to hire a ghostwriter to help him write his memoirs.

    (A) Being not a writer himself, the champion golfer

    (B) Being not a writer, the champion golfer

    (C) The champion golfer, being not a writer himself,

    (D) The champion golfer, who was not a writer,

    (E) The champion golfer, who was not himself a writer,

31. Although he gave an impassioned closing speech, <u>the lawyer whom the defendant's parents had hired is going to be unable to</u> sway the jury, which returned a guilty verdict.

    (A) the lawyer whom the defendant's parents had hired is going to be unable to

    (B) the lawyer whom the defendant's parents had hired was unable to

    (C) the lawyer who the defendant's parents had hired was unable to

    (D) the lawyer who the defendant's parents had hired is going to be unable to

    (E) the lawyer who the defendant's parents had hired is not going to be able to

32. The doctor instructed his patient <u>not to engage in strenuous exercise or otherwise tax the affected</u> muscle.

    (A) not to engage in strenuous exercise or otherwise tax the affected

    (B) not to engage in strenuous exercise or otherwise to tax the effected

    (C) neither to engage in strenuous exercise or otherwise tax the affected

    (D) either to engage in strenuous exercise nor otherwise tax the affected

    (E) neither to engage in strenuous exercise nor otherwise tax the effected

33. Before athletes are allowed onto the national team, <u>they must first demonstrate a willingness to accept humble accommodations, spartan training regimes, and to limit contact with loved ones</u>.

    (A) they must first demonstrate a willingness to accept humble accommodations, spartan training regimes, and to limit contact with loved ones

    (B) they must first demonstrate a willingness to accept humble accommodations, spartan training regimes, and limited contact with loved ones

    (C) they must first demonstrate a willingness to accept humble accommodations, spartan training regimes, and limiting contact with loved ones

    (D) he or she must first demonstrate a willingness to accept humble accommodations, spartan training regimes, and to limit contact with loved ones

    (E) he or she must first demonstrate a willingness to accept humble accommodations, spartan training regimes, and limited contact with loved ones

34. Before turning to the literary pursuits that would make him famous, <u>painting was Samuel Butler's choice of study</u>.

    (A) painting was Samuel Butler's choice of study

    (B) painting was being Samuel Butler's choice of study

    (C) Samuel Butler was choosing to study painting

    (D) Samuel Butler has chosen to study painting

    (E) Samuel Butler studied painting

35. In overpopulated cities with congested streets, walking has become <u>a more popular mode of transport than to drive</u>.

    (A) a more popular mode of transport than to drive

    (B) a more popular mode of transport than driving

    (C) more popular than to drive for transport

    (D) more popular as a mode of transport than to drive

    (E) the most popular form of transport

GO ON TO THE NEXT PAGE

36. Although tulips are our favorite flowers, <u>we decided not to plant any this year because we feared attracting deer</u>.

    (A) we decided not to plant any this year because we feared attracting deer
    (B) we decided not to plant them this year because attracting deer was a fear
    (C) we decided not to plant any this year because of the fear of attracting deer
    (D) our fear of attracting deer was the reason we decided not to plant any this year
    (E) this year our fear was attracting deer

37. <u>Due to the fact that bicycles and scooters have become very popular is why some cities are allowing their use in bus lanes.</u>
    (A) Due to the fact that bicycles and scooters have become very popular is why some cities are allowing their use in bus lanes.
    (B) Because bicycles, and scooters, are popularizing, some cities allow their use in bus lanes.
    (C) Because bicyles and scooters have become very popular, some cities are allowing their use in bus lanes.
    (D) Due to the fact that bicycles and scooters are popularizing, some cities are allowing their use in bus lanes.
    (E) Consequent to their popularity, some cities are allowing bicycles and scooters in bus lanes.

38. <u>Complying with demands made by the United Nations, the belligerent country withdrew its armaments from neighboring countries.</u>

    (A) Complying with demands made by the United Nations, the belligerent country withdrew its armaments from neighboring countries.
    (B) Complying with demands made by the United Nations, the belligerent country withdrew their armaments from neighboring countries.
    (C) Complying to demands made by the United Nations, the belligerent country withdrew their armaments from neighboring countries.
    (D) Complying with demands made by the United Nations, the armaments were withdrawn by the belligerent country from their neighboring countries.
    (E) Complying with demands made by the United Nations, neighboring countries no longer housed the armaments of the belligerent country.

GO ON TO THE NEXT PAGE

WRITING TEST

Directions: Each of the following passages is an early draft of an essay. Some parts of the passages need to be rewritten.

Read each passage and answer the questions that follow. Some questions are about particular sentences or parts of sentences and ask you to improve sentence structure and word choice. Other questions refer to parts of the essay or the entire essay and ask you to consider organization and development. In making your decisions, follow the conventions of standard written English. After you have chosen your answer, fill in the corresponding oval on your answer sheet.

Questions 39–44 are based on the following passage.

(1) *The law is responsible for licensing and restricting many things, among them driving and voting.* (2) *Most people support the age restrictions our country has placed on these two activities, which is good, and very few have thought to regulate parenting.* (3) *For instance, the reason one can't vote before a certain age is that your opinion would be considered irresponsible.*

(4) *So shouldn't parents also be a certain age before they can have children?* (5) *This demands a more theoretical than practical response, because of course there is no way to apply the law to giving birth.* (6) *That doesn't mean, however, that there aren't things we can't do to encourage people to be more responsible when it comes to parenting.*

(7) *The practice of young people having kids is a problem not only for the children who suffer from immature parents but also for the grandparents who are often left with babysitting and financial burdens.* (8) *The other people who suffer from having children too young are the actual parents.* (9) *Educational opportunities often get pushed aside and low level jobs are taken because the demands of rent and child costs must come first.*

(10) *There is the legacy factor also.* (11) *Numerous statistics show that if you are born to very young parents, you are more likely to have your own children at a young age.* (12) *If you haven't had a chance to get your own education and mature sufficiently, how could one be a good parent to your child?* (13) *Sometimes love isn't enough.*

39. Which of the following would be the most suitable replacement for "*and*" in sentence 2 (reproduced below)?

Most people support the age restrictions our country has placed on these two activities, which is good, and very few have thought to regulate parenting.

(A) consequently
(B) but
(C) additionally
(D) while
(E) perhaps

40. The function of sentence 4 is to

(A) establish a claim that contradicts the passage's argument
(B) set up a hypothetical situation
(C) challenge a commonly held belief about raising children
(D) pose a question to which the answer is implied
(E) illustrate the writer's confusion

41. In context, adding which of the following words after "*This*" would make sentence 5 more precise ?

(A) claim
(B) example
(C) question
(D) situation
(E) law

GO ON TO THE NEXT PAGE

42. Which of the following sentences is best inserted at the beginning of the third paragraph, before sentence 7 ?

    (A) Although there currently aren't laws to prevent young people from giving birth, there should be.
    (B) Examples of the consequences of having children at a very early age are many and significant for both children and parents.
    (C) One way to encourage responsibility is to point out how giving birth at a young age can negatively affect families.
    (D) Many statistics point to the difficulty young parents have when raising children.
    (E) How would you feel if your parents were too young to support you properly?

43. Which of the following options is the best way to combine sentences 10 and 11 (reproduced below)?

    There is the legacy factor also. Numerous statistics show that if you are born to very young parents, you are more likely to have your own children at a young age.

    (A) Numerous statistics also point to a legacy factor: being born to very young parents increases one's likelihood of having children at a young age.
    (B) The legacy factor also shows statistically that if one is born to very young parents, one increases one's likelihood of having one's own children at a young age.
    (C) The legacy factor is also shown in numerous statistics showing that if you are born to very young parents, you are likely to have your own children at a young age.
    (D) Numerous statistics show that if you are born to very young parents, you are more likely to have your children at a young age and to consider the legacy factor.
    (E) The legacy factor shows numerous statistics as well that are showing that if you are born to very young parents, you are more likely to have your own children at a young age.

44. Which of the following revisions of the underlined portion of sentence 14 (reproduced below) is best?

    If you haven't had a chance to get your own education and mature sufficiently, how could one be a good parent to your child?

    (A) a child doesn't have a chance to get their own education and maturation, how could he or she
    (B) a child doesn't get an education and to have a chance to mature, how could he or she
    (C) you haven't educated or matured yourself , how could they
    (D) you had not had the chance to mature, how will you in the future
    (E) you haven't had an education or the chance to mature, how can you

GO ON TO THE NEXT PAGE

Questions 45–50 are based on the following passage.

(1) *In reading* Othello, *I became aware that it was not only one of the best plays I ever read but its characters were complex and enjoyable. (2) Readers become emotionally involved with them. (3) They would want Iago to be found out by any of the people he has duped. (4) The play can be enjoyed by readers just as a suspenseful play; or as a symbol.*

(5) *Shakespeare uses multiple symbols in his play. (6) Many readers feel Iago is so extreme in his scheming that he represents complete evil. (7) But simple symbols can be boring, which is why Shakespeare complicated Iago by making him human with motives such as ambition and lust. (8) Othello is also complex, being that he represents the struggle of the good man at heart against the foolish one who is swayed by the forces of evil. (9) Although Desdemona, the symbol of purity, dies tragically, Shakespeare's vision is not depressing, the evildoers are eventually punished.*

(10) *Meanwhile, the readers have enjoyed the dramatic suspense. (11) There are myriad twists and turns and Iago is one of those characters that readers love to hate. (12) The language that Iago uses is rich and true to his character. (13) In fact, the extent to which it is rich and true is so great that many readers don't want him to be caught too early in the play. (14) The most interesting writing is that which is complex and which also explores human nature in a way that we can all relate to. (15) For this reason, I would have to choose* Othello *as a book I would recommend to anyone who hasn't had the pleasure of reading him.*

45. In context, which of the following revisions does sentence 2 need most?

    (A) Change "them" to "the characters".
    (B) Change "involved" to "concerned".
    (C) Omit "emotionally".
    (D) Insert "and the plot" at the end.
    (E) Insert "Furthermore" at the beginning.

46. Which of the following is the best revision of sentence 4 (reproduced below)?

The play can be enjoyed by readers just as a suspenseful play; or as a symbol.

    (A) (As it is now)
    (B) Readers can enjoy the play for its suspense or for its symbolism.
    (C) The play, which can be appreciated as a suspenseful play or a symbolic play, is enjoyable either way.
    (D) You can enjoy the play's suspense or its symbols.
    (E) Both the suspense and the symbols are aspects of the play that you can enjoy.

47. Sentence 5 functions as

    (A) the passage's central argument
    (B) the topic statement for the second paragraph
    (C) the argument that the writer wants to refute in the second paragraph
    (D) the conclusion of the second paragraph
    (E) a brief digression from the passage's topic

GO ON TO THE NEXT PAGE

48. Which of the following revisions of the underlined portion of sentence 8 (reproduced below) is best?

    Othello is also complex, being that he represents the struggle of the good man at heart against the foolish one who is swayed by the forces of evil.

    (A) Othello is also complex, being that he represented
    (B) Othello, complex also, is represented by
    (C) Being complex, Othello also represents
    (D) Othello is also complex; he represents
    (E) Othello's complexity also represents

49. Which of the following is the best revision of the underlined portion of sentence 9 (reproduced below)?

    Although Desdemona, the symbol of purity, dies tragically, Shakespeare's vision is not depressing, the evildoers are eventually punished.

    (A) depressing, despite the evildoers' eventual punishment
    (B) depressing, although punishment eventually comes to the evildoers
    (C) depressing; consequently, the evildoers are punished
    (D) depressing, but the evildoers are eventually punished
    (E) depressing, since the evildoers are eventually punished

50. Which of the following sentences best combines sentences 12 and 13 (reproduced below)?

    The language that Iago uses is rich and true to his character. In fact, the extent to which it is rich and true is so great that many readers don't want him to be caught too early in the play.

    (A) In fact, because of the rich and true language Iago uses, many readers do not catch him early in the play.
    (B) Many readers, being greatly appreciative of the richness and trueness of Iago's language, don't want him to be caught too early in the play.
    (C) It is so great how rich and true Iago's language is, and consequently many readers don't want him to be caught too early in the play.
    (D) Iago's language is so rich and so true to his character that many readers don't want him to be caught too early in the play.
    (E) The extent to which the language of Iago is rich and true is great, and many readers as a result wish that he would not be caught too early in the play.

GO ON TO THE NEXT PAGE

WRITING TEST

51. After moving to the rural countryside, the girl, who
        A   B

   had always lived in polluted cities, said she was
        C

   relieved to breath fresh air. No error
                   D   E

52. The two friends that went to high school with Nick are
                    A

   thinking of joining him on a cross-country trip.
      B   C   D

   No error
      E

53. The biology book that the teachers initially gave us
                                        A

   was replaced recently by one with illustrations that
                         B   C

   made the new book easier to understand than its
                                                 D

   predecessor. No error
                E

54. When the young girl Marnie realized that she had
            A   B

   gotten less pieces of candy than her sister, she threw
          C   D

   a temper tantrum. No error
                    E

55. If she had been able to nail the back flip at the
       A

   gymnastics championship, she will win the gold
                               B

   medal, and her main rival would have come in second.
          C   D

   No error
      E

56. Unable to handle much criticism, Lesley angrily
                       A   B

   opposed any point of view that differed from her.
                              C   D

   No error
      E

57. In the year 1973, the Supreme Court ruled that
        A   B

   advertisements for employment could no longer specify
                    C   D

   gender. No error
           E

GO ON TO THE NEXT PAGE

WRITING TEST—*Continued*

58. <u>Due</u> to <u>its</u> hardy nature and perennial blooms, azalea
    A   B

    shrubs have been <u>cultivated</u> in hybrid forms for <u>much</u>
                  C   D

    of the last century. <u>No error</u>
                      E

59. The trustee, <u>whom</u> the court had appointed many years
              A

    earlier, <u>was</u> eventually replaced by a less gracious <u>but</u>
        B   C

    <u>equally</u> competent member of the family. <u>No error</u>
     D   E

60. Aggressive angles and precise details <u>are</u>
                                        A

    characteristic <u>of</u> Kandinsky's work and <u>has been</u>
                   B   C

    imitated by generations of artists <u>around</u> the world.
                                     D

    <u>No error</u>
      E

S T O P

IF YOU FINISH BEFORE TIME IS CALLED, YOU MAY CHECK YOUR WORK ON THIS TEST ONLY.
DO NOT TURN TO ANY OTHER TEST IN THIS BOOK.

SAT II Writing
Practice Test 4
Explanations

Calculating Your Score

Question Number	Correct Answer	Right	Wrong	Question Number	Correct Answer	Right	Wrong
1.	D	——	——	31.	B	——	——
2.	E	——	——	32.	A	——	——
3.	A	——	——	33.	B	——	——
4.	C	——	——	34.	E	——	——
5.	C	——	——	35.	B	——	——
6.	E	——	——	36.	A	——	——
7.	C	——	——	37.	C	——	——
8.	B	——	——	38.	A	——	——
9.	E	——	——	39.	B	——	——
10.	D	——	——	40.	D	——	——
11.	D	——	——	41.	C	——	——
12.	D	——	——	42.	C	——	——
13.	A	——	——	43.	A	——	——
14.	E	——	——	44.	E	——	——
15.	D	——	——	45.	A	——	——
16.	B	——	——	46.	B	——	——
17.	C	——	——	47.	B	——	——
18.	D	——	——	48.	D	——	——
19.	C	——	——	49.	E	——	——
20.	D	——	——	50.	D	——	——
21.	A	——	——	51.	D	——	——
22.	D	——	——	52.	A	——	——
23.	E	——	——	53.	E	——	——
24.	C	——	——	54.	C	——	——
25.	B	——	——	55.	B	——	——
26.	B	——	——	56.	D	——	——
27.	A	——	——	57.	A	——	——
28.	D	——	——	58.	B	——	——
29.	B	——	——	59.	E	——	——
30.	D	——	——	60.	C	——	——

Your raw score for the SAT II Writing test is a composite of your raw score in the multiple-choice section and your score on the essay. Once you have determined your composite score, use the conversion table on pages 16-17 to calculate your scaled score. To calculate your raw score, count the number of questions you answered correctly on the multiple choice: _____
A

Count the number of questions you answered incorrectly, and multiply that number by $\frac{1}{4}$:

$$\underline{\hspace{2cm}} \times \frac{1}{4} = \underline{\hspace{2cm}}$$
B   C

Subtract the value in field C from value in field A: _____
D

Round the number to the nearest whole number: _____
E

Take your score for the essay (ask a teacher to grade your essay or grade yourself) and multiply it by 3.43:

$$\underline{\hspace{2cm}} \times 3.43 = \underline{\hspace{2cm}}$$
F   G

Add the number in field E to the number in Field G: _____
H

Round the number in field H. This is your SAT II Writing score: _____

Student Essays

Total Score: 12 (each reader gave the essay a 6)

Cases of human survival demonstrate the truth of the expression "necessity is the mother of invention." Often when people face life-threatening situations, they display remarkable courage and creativity in their struggles to survive against the odds. You can find examples of these survival stories in both literature and reality. In the novel Robinson Crusoe, *Daniel Defoe describes Crusoe's inventive survival skills when he is shipwrecked on a remote island. And only recently in real life, a man trapped in a car at the bottom of a ravine used the trash around him to stay alive for almost a week.*

Robinson Crusoe *portrays a man who uses a few tools and a great deal of ingenuity to create a civilized life on a remote island. At the beginning of the novel, Defoe portrays Crusoe as a reckless, irresponsible youth who defies his father. The young Crusoe refuses to settle down to a respectable life in his native town and sets out, hoping to make his fortune at sea. The reader gets the sense that Crusoe has little knowledge about the realities of everyday life and that his head is full of adventure. After Crusoe is shipwrecked alone on an island, though, his character begins to change out of necessity, as he settles the island in order to suvive. Immediately after the shipwreck, Crusoe performs his first act of ingenuity: he builds a raft out of broken lumber to take him out to the shipwreck. There he gathers as many supplies as he can before the ship sinks. Using these salvaged tools, he constructs a shelter near the shore and captures a goat. As his skills develop, he expands and fortifies his home and builds a boat he uses for expeditions. During his time on the island, Crusoe's life becomes increasingly settled and starts to resemble the civilized English life he left behind. He domesticates animals (a parrot and goat), and he furnishes his home with the woven baskets and pieces of pottery he has taught himself to make.*

The media recently reported a story about a modern day Robinson Crusoe. A man drove his car into a ravine in West Virginia. The crash broke the man's hip and left the car so destroyed that the horn and headlights stopped working. The man was pinned in his car with no way to crawl out or signal for help. Instead of giving up in despair, he used the trash in his car to survive for six days until the rescuers finally came. For sustenance, he drunk the Taco Bell sauce packets scattered on the floor and ate old peanut butter. He made fires out of tissue scraps to keep himself warm and to melt snow so he could drink water. And he ripped out the car's lining to use as a blanket in the near-freezing temperatures.

These survival stories show how people can overcome dire situations relying almost solely on their wits. It takes real ingenuity to survive on bits of trash, and it takes real necessity to push one to this kind of desperation. To me, the greatest lesson that these stories teach is that people don't need modern conveniences. Put to the test, humans can survive on very little.

Discussion:

While this essay has a few problems, overall it demonstrates clear and consistent competence. The writer addresses the topic effectively through good examples, organization, and prose.

In the introduction, the writer presents an argument and describes the evidence that supports it. The writer chooses to define invention as human inventiveness rather than as findings or discoveries, and says that survival stories demonstrate the truth of "necessity is the mother of invention."

The two examples the writer uses are *Robinson Crusoe* and a recent incident involving a man trapped in a ravine. In the second paragraph, the writer expands the discussion of *Robinson Crusoe*, describing how Crusoe settled the island where he was shipwrecked using his creativity and some supplies from the ship.

The third paragraph focuses on the man who was trapped in his car. The details in this paragraph are vivid, and the subject is a good one, since the writer demonstrates an awareness of current events.

As with most essays, the conclusion is the weakest part. The writer avoids simply rehashing the passage's argument, but the statement *to me, the greatest lesson that these stories teach is that people don't need modern conveniences* seems to come a little out of the blue.

The essay's main technical problems are repetition and a couple of grammatical mistakes. The second and third paragraphs feel choppy because the sentences vary little in structure. In the second paragraph, most of the sentences are in the form *he builds . . . , he gathers . . .,* and *he constructs . . . .* The writer could have improved the flow of the sentences by varying their structure somewhat. In the third paragraph, the writer makes a couple of grammatical errors. The sentence *He drunk the Taco Bell sauce packets* gets the verb tense of *to drink* wrong. The sentence should say that he *drank* the sauce packets. The last sentence in the paragraph begins with *and.* While starting a sentence with a conjunction like *and, but,* or *yet* is common in everyday speech, it's not acceptable in formal English.

None of these problems are great enough to detract from the essay's score. The clear argument and the effective use of evidence earn it a perfect score of 12.

Total Score: 4 (each reader gave the essay a 2)

Necessity is the mother of invention. This statement is correct for many reasons, and I will talk about some of them now. The reason that people invent is because they have a need. Usually, maybe not always, the need is very strong. For example, people invented the wheel to help them carry things, which is an important part of life even if people don't think about it alot. Even in places where women carried things on top of there heads, something like a wheel would have made life easier. Imagine carrying water all day long just so you will have enough to drink and wash your clothes! Wheels would make life simpler, especially when they are used to make things like shopping carts and cars which make carrying things much more convenient. Then you could pay more attention to your children and not to carrying water.

If people didn't need things, they wouldn't have invented them. Why else would we have electricity? If we didn't have it, we wouldn't have any lights, TV, etc., people would go to bed earlier and not do as much at night. (Which may be a good thing but that is another topic.) We can solve all problems by putting our heads to them.

In conclusion, we don't invent anything we don't need. Look around you, at the supermarket or on the bus, and you'll see the many things we invented to satisfy needs.

Discussion:

This writer uses some good examples to back up the argument that necessity is in fact the mother of invention, but the essay loses points because of its poor organization, its weak development of the examples, and its multiple grammatical errors.

Poor organization, particularly the lack of a separate introduction, weakens the essay. The introductory statements and the first example (the wheel) are all crammed into the first paragraph. The writer begins unoriginally, restating the essay topic: *necessity is the mother of invention.* The next sentence, which says that the statement is correct and that the writer will discuss why, is unnecessary, since its sole purpose is to state what readers will assume: that the writer will back up the argument with evidence in the essay. Then the writer shifts to a discussion about the wheel and its benefits.

Splitting this first paragraph into two paragraphs would improve the essay's organization. The first paragraph should be an introduction, which presents the essay's argument and summarizes the supporting evidence used in the essay: the inventions of the wheel and of electricity. A detailed explanation of the wheel example does not belong in the introduction. Instead, it should be the sole focus of the second paragraph.

In terms of organization, the second and third paragraphs are okay. The second paragraph focuses on the invention of electricty, and the third paragraph is the essay's conclusion. The main problem with the second paragraph is the lack of development. Whereas the writer tries to develop the wheel example, explaining how the wheel makes carrying things less time consuming (and presumably less energy consuming), the writer does little to expand the electricity example. All the writer says is that electricity resulted in the invention of lights and television, but he gives little sense of the necessity for these items.

On top of these organization and content problems, the writer makes many grammatical mistakes and uses awkward prose. Among these errors are a couple of wrong words in the first paragraph: *alot* instead of *a lot* (or preferably *much*) and *there* instead of the possessive pronoun *their*. The second paragraph contains a run-on sentence (*If we didn't have it, we wouldn't have any lights, TV, etc., people would go to bed earlier and not do as much at night*) and a fragment (*Which may be a good thing but that is another topic*). The abbreviations *TV* and *etc.* should not be used in formal essays. The writer should change *TV* to *television* and drop *etc.* from the essay.

In the end, the examples (however undeveloped they are) save the essay from getting the lowest possible score. Coming up with the examples of the wheel and electricity shows some creativity and some knowledge of history on the writer's part and counteracts, to a minor extent, all of the other problems with the essay.

Identifying Sentence Errors

1. **(D)** *Redundancy*

Redundancy errors are hard to catch because they're made frequently in speech. In this sentence, the phrases *in addition to* and *as well* are redundant because they serve the same function. You can fix this error by taking out *as well*.

2. **(E)** *No Error*

No error.

3. **(A)** *Subject-Verb Agreement*

Percentage is a singular noun, so the verb that follows it should be the singular *has* instead of the plural *have*. Subject-verb agreement can be tricky when the subject and verb are separated by a prepositional phrase like *of teenagers who smoke*. Because *teenagers* is a plural noun, the plural verb *have* may look right, but you need to remember that the subject of the sentence is the singular *percentage*.

4. **(C)** *Pronoun Agreement*

Since *the parks commission* is a singular noun phrase, the pronoun that modifies it should be the singular *its* rather than the plural *their*.

5. **(C)** *Diction*

Either/or and *neither/nor* are exclusive pairings. In other words, *or* must follow *either* and *nor* must follow *neither*. To correct this sentence, replace *nor* with *or*. The sentence should say, *either his security detail or the local police.*

6. **(E)** *No Error*

No error.

7. **(C)**   *Subject-Verb Agreement*

Spotting subject-verb agreement errors can be difficult when the verb comes before the subject. In this sentence, the verb is the singular *was*, and the subject is the plural compound noun *the owner's tabby cat and three nursing kittens*. In order to fix the agreement error, you need to change the verb to the plural *were*.

8. **(B)**   *Tense*

You'll probably catch this verb tense error with your ear because the infinitive verb *to be* sounds funny. Emily was accustomed to *being* mistaken, not *to be* mistaken.

9. **(E)**   *No Error*

No error.

10. **(D)**   *Wrong Word*

Indecisive is the wrong word in this sentence because it means unable to decide and is usually applied to people, not periods of time. The right word is probably either *undetermined*, which means not yet decided, or *indeterminate*, which means not decided in advance.

11. **(D)**   *Double Negative*

Not hardly is a classic double negative: two consecutive negative words that cancel each other out. The phrase *not hardly as high as they should have been* actually means that they *were* as high as they should have been. You can fix this error by getting rid of the word *hardly*.

12. **(D)**   *Pronoun Case*

In this sentence, the noun *peers* is compared to the pronoun *them*: *the peers . . . are held in higher esteem than them*. In a comparison involving a noun and a pronoun, the pronoun needs to be in the same case as the noun. The easiest way to figure out the correct case of the pronoun is to complete the sentence using a verb: *the peers are held in higher esteem than them are*. Since *them are* is wrong, you should switch the pronoun to *they*: *the peers are held in higher esteem than they are*.

13. **(A)**   *Wrong Word*

To rise means to get up, whereas *to raise* means to lift something. This sentence states that the store increases the prices, so the correct verb is *to raise*.

14. **(E)**   *No Error*

No error.

15. **(D)**   *Idiom*

This sentence makes an idiom error, which you'll probably catch with your ear. The expression *make up in personality what he lacked through skill* violates the rules of English. The correct expression is *make up in personality what he lacked in skill*. You may have thought that *by far* seems redundant, but *by far* is used to emphasize the degree to which Paul is weaker than his teammates.

16. **(B)**   *Tense*

The verb tenses in this sentence are complicated, but you'll probably notice that *be changing* sounds funny after *might not*. The verbs *had had*, *might*, and *would have stayed* are in the past tense, but *be changing* is in the present. The sentence should say *if he had had a good time, the tourist might not have changed*.

17. (C) _Wrong Word_

Effect is usually a noun, and it means the result of something. _Affect_ is usually a verb, and it means to change or influence something. In this sentence, which says that construction would change traffic patterns, _affect_ is the right word to use.

18. (D) _Conjunction_

The conjunction _and_ incorrectly links the dependent clause _Although many people once believed..._ to the independent clause _there is now a theory...._ Conjunctions, such as _and_, _but_, or _or_, should connect two independent clauses (clauses that can function as complete sentences on their own). To fix this error, you should replace _and_ with a comma: _Although many people once believed that Tchaikovsky died from cholera, there is now a theory that he died by committing suicide._

19. (C) _Pronoun Shift_

This sentence incorrectly shifts from talking about you to talking about one. Since both of these pronouns refer to the same person, you need to choose one of them and use it consistently. In this case, change _one_ to _you_, since _one_ is underlined and _you_ is not.

20. (D) _Faulty Comparison_

This sentence compares the _underdog's grassroots campaign_ to the underdog's _rival_. This comparison is wrong: you can't compare a campaign to a man. A correct comparison sets the _underdog's campaign_ against _his rival's campaign_, or just _his rival's_.

Improving Sentence Errors

21. (A) _No Error_

No error.

22. (D) _Idiom_

The original sentence makes an idiom error when it says that the idea of a meritocracy is _as appealing than it is difficult._ In English, the correct expression is that something is _as appealing as it is difficult._ Choices (C), (D), and (E) fix the idiom error, but (C) and (E) make other errors. Choice (C) commits faulty parallelism by changing the verb _is_ to _can be_: _as appealing as it can be difficult._ Choice (E) makes a pronoun agreement error when it uses a plural pronoun, _they_, to modify the single noun phrase, _the idea of a meritocracy_. Thus (D) is the right answer.

23. (E) _Misplaced Modifier_

The original sentence has a misplaced modifier. The words _the fact_ immediately follow the opening clause, _while concealing the fact that she had drawn a spade._ This arrangement implies that the fact had done the concealing, but what the sentence wants to say is that _the professional gambler_ concealed that she had drawn a spade. To fix the sentence, you need to place _the professional gambler_ directly after the opening clause. Choices (C), (D), and (E) make this change, but (C) doesn't state that the gambler hid the duplicate set of cards, and (D) makes a tense error when it switches from the past tense (_the gambler drew_) to the present tense (_she hides_). (E), the remaining answer choice, is correct.

24. **(C)** *Subject-Verb Agreement*

The original sentence contains a subject-verb agreement error. Since *none* is a singular noun, it should be followed by a singular verb, *was*, instead of a plural verb, *were*. You can eliminate (A) and (B) because they make this agreement error. Although (D) corrects the agreement error, it uses an incorrect idiom: *regardless to* instead of *regardless of*. (E) also corrects the agreement error, but it turns the sentence into a fragment by adding *who*. Choice (C) is the correct answer.

25. **(B)** *Fragment*

The original sentence is not really a sentence at all; it's a fragment, lacking an independent clause. The subject of the sentence is *the board of directors*, and the main verb is *moving*, but verbs that end in *-ing* aren't strong enough to make complete sentences. In order to form a complete sentence, you need to change *moving* to *moved*: *the company's board of directors quickly moved to cut costs.*

26. **(B)** *Parallelism*

More often than not, lists on the SAT II Writing contain parallelism errors. This list has two gerunds (words that end in *-ing*) followed by *how to use the Internet*. According to the rules of parallelism, all of the items in this list must be in the same form, so you need to convert *how to use the Internet* into a gerund. The correct answer is choice (B), which changes the underlined portion of the sentence to *on typing, word processing, and using the Internet.*

27. **(A)** *No Error*

No error.

28. **(D)** *Run-on*

The original sentence is a run-on. Its two independent clauses—*It was the governor's suggestion that*... and *that way he could*...—are jammed together with only a comma between them, but a comma isn't strong enough to hold them together on its own. These two clauses could very well be two sentences, but the answer choices ask you to combine them into a single, grammatically correct sentence. The correct answer, (D), fixes the run-on by making one of the clauses dependent on the other. The sentence in (D) shows why the governor suggested that his campaign manager take time off: so the campaign manager could recharge his batteries.

29. **(B)** *Subject-Verb Agreement*

Neither is one of those singular nouns that looks plural but in reality is singular. In the original sentence, the singular subject *neither of the two doctors* is followed by a plural verb, *are seeking*. Choices (B), (C), and (D) change the plural *are seeking* to the singular *is seeking*, but (C) and (D) incorrectly insert a plural pronoun, *their*, to modify *neither*. Choice (B) avoids this mistake by not using a pronoun, and it's the correct answer.

30. **(D)** *Other*

The main problem with the original sentence is its wordiness. On the SAT II Writing, you should almost always get rid of gerunds (words that end in *-ing*) if you're given the choice. Choices (D) and (E) rewrite the original sentence without the clunky phrase that begins with *being*. Both (D) and (E) improve the sentence's clarity, but choice (D) is a better answer than (E) because it cuts down on wordiness. If you need to choose between two answers that both seem correct, you should almost always go with the shorter one. (Remember that this method is not surefire, but it generally works.) Since choice (D) makes sense without the pronoun *himself*, it is the best answer.

31. (B)   *Tense*

The underlined part of the original sentence contains a tense error. Since the rest of the sentence is in the past tense (*he gave* and *which returned*), the underlined section also needs to be in the past tense. *Whom the defendant's parents had hired* is in the past tense, but the *lawyer . . . is going* is not. In order to correct the sentence, you need to change *is going* to *was*: *the lawyer was unable to sway*. Choices (B) and (C) fix the tense error, but (C) incorrectly uses the pronoun *who* instead of *whom*. If you have trouble remembering which is which, try replacing *who* with *he* and *whom* with *him*. *The parents had hired he* sounds funny, but *the parents had hired him* sounds right, so you know that *whom* is the correct word in this case and that (B) is correct.

32. (A)   *No Error*

No error.

33. (B)   *Parallelism*

Whenever you see a list on the SAT II Writing, you should look out for a parallelism error. In the original sentence, the first two items in the list are noun phrases: *a willingness to accept humble accommodations* and *spartan training regimes*. The third item, though, is a verb phrase: *to limit contact with loved ones*. To fix this parallelism error, you should replace the verb phrase with a noun phrase like *limited contact with loved ones*. Choices (B) and (E) make this change, but (E) makes a pronoun agreement error by modifying the plural noun *athletes* with the singular pronoun phrase *his or her*.

34. (E)   *Misplaced Modifier*

Because of a misplaced modifier, the original sentence implies that painting, not Butler, turned to literary pursuits. To fix this error, you need to place Butler directly next to the modifier: *Before turning to the literary pursuits that would make him famous, Samuel Butler studied painting*.

35. (B)   *Parallelism*

The original sentence compares the gerund *walking* to the infinitive *to drive*, thus violating the rules of parallelism. You need to change the sentence to compare either gerund to gerund or infinitive to infinitive. If you read through the answer choices, you'll see that choice (B) replaces *to drive* with *driving* and creates a parallel sentence.

36. (A)   *No Error*

No error.

37. (C)   *Other*

Do you get the feeling that this sentence takes a while to make its point? If you do, you're right. The sentence has a bad case of wordiness. Get rid of the awkward phrases *due to the fact* and *is why*, and set up a straightforward sentence using *because*. Choices (B) and (C) use the *because* arrangement, but (B) incorrectly changes *have become very popular* to *are popularizing*. To popularize means to cater to popular tastes, not to be popular, so choice (C) is the right answer.

38. (A)   *No Error*

No error.

Improving Paragraphs

39. (B) *Revision*

In order to answer this question, you need to figure out the relationship between the part of the sentence before *and* the part of the sentence after it. The first part of the sentence says that most people support regulation for driving and voting, and the second part says that few people think about regulating parenting. These two ideas are in contrast to each other, so you need a transitional word that suggests difference. Of the answer choices, choice (B), *but*, works best in the sentence's context.

40. (D) *Analysis*

Sentence 4 is what's called a rhetorical question, and the writer uses it for effect. The question doesn't expect an answer because the answer is supposed to be not only implied but also self-evident.

41. (C) *Addition*

This refers to the question asked in the previous sentence, so the addition of *question* would make sentence 5 more precise.

42. (C) *Addition*

Answering this addition question requires some analysis of the second and third paragraphs. The sentence that you insert before sentence 7 should serve as both a transition between the second and third paragraphs and the topic statement of the third. At the end of the second paragraph, the writer suggests that there are ways of discouraging young people from parenthood. The third paragraph describes how various people suffer when young people have to raise their children. Choice (C), the best answer choice, links the two paragraphs by saying that the negative aspects of young parenthood could be used to dissuade young people from having children.

43. (A) *Combining Sentences*

Sentence 10 mentions a legacy factor, and sentence 11 describes what the legacy factor is. Choice (A), the correct answer, is somewhat unusual for the SAT II Writing because it uses a colon to combine the two sentences. The first part of choice (A) brings up the legacy factor, and the second part explains what the legacy factor is. (A) also rephrases sentence 10 to get rid of the passive-sounding *there is*, saying instead that *numerous statistics point to a legacy factor*.

44. (E) *Revision*

The original sentence shifts from using the pronoun *you* to using the pronoun *one*, even though *you* and *one* are supposed to refer to the same person. In order to fix this error, you need to make the pronouns consistent: use either *you* or *one* exclusively. Choices (D) and (E) turn all of the pronouns in the sentence into *you*, but in addition to being wordy, (D) uses inconsistent (and weird) tenses: *had not had* and *will be*. Choice (E) is the best revision of the original sentence.

45. (A) *Revision*

Sentence 2 says that *readers become emotionally involved with them*, but doesn't make it clear who *them* is. Of course, if you look at sentence 1, you'll probably assume that *them* refers to the *characters* in Othello, but you can't be sure that *them* doesn't refer to the other plural noun, *plays*. In order to make sentence 2 more precise, you should replace *them* with *the characters*.

46. (B) *Revision*

Sentence 4 is wrong because it uses a semicolon to separate a dependent clause (*or as a symbol*) from an independent clause (*the play can be enjoyed...*). Semicolons connect independent clauses to each other, but they are too "strong" for dependent clauses (clauses that can't function as sentences on their own). Since the original sentence is wrong, you can rule out choice (A). Of the remaining answer choices, (C) and (E) are wordy, and (D) introduces *you* into the sentence. Choice (B) is the best answer.

47. (B) *Analysis*

Sentence 5, which states that Shakespeare uses many symbols in his play, is the topic sentence of the second paragraph. In this paragraph, the writer gives examples of symbols used in *Othello*: Iago is the symbol of evil and Desdemona of purity.

48. (D) *Revision*

The phrase *being that* makes the original sentence seem awkward and wordy. Read through the answer choices to find the best revision. Choice (A), which changes *represents* to *represented*, doesn't improve the sentence at all. Choice (B) uses the passive voice (*Othello is represented*), which you should avoid like the plague on the SAT II Writing. Choice (C) uses the clumsy gerund *being*. Generally, if you have the option of getting rid of *being* and other *-ing* words, you should take it. You may feel nervous about choice (D) because it splits the sentence with a semicolon, but it is clear and grammatically correct. Choice (E) also seems clear and concise, but it changes the meaning of the sentence. The original sentence says that Othello represents the struggle between good and evil, but (E) states that Othello's *complexity* represents this struggle. Of the answer choices, (D) is the best revision.

49. (E) *Revision*

Sentence 9 incorrectly uses a comma to connect two independent clauses: *Shakespeare's vision is not depressing* and *the evildoers are eventually punished*. Each of the answer choices tries to fix the run-on by adding an adverb or conjunction. You need to figure out which of these words makes the most sense in the context of the sentence. Choice (E) is the best revision of the original sentence. It is grammatically correct, and the adverb *since* explains why Shakespeare's vision is not depressing: because the bad guys are punished in the end.

50. (D) *Combining Sentences*

The first part of sentence 13 basically repeats what sentence 12 said: that Iago's language is rich and true to his character. You should condense these two sentences into a single one that says that readers don't want Iago to be caught early in the play because he's such a great character. Of the answer choices, (D) does the best job of combining the sentences, using the structure *so . . . that . . . .* Choices (B) and (E) have similar meanings to (D), but they are very wordy.

Identifying Sentence Errors

51. (D) *Wrong Word*

Breath is a noun, as in "take a breath of fresh air." *Breathe* is a verb, as in "I breathe fresh air." The tiny letter *e* makes a big difference. The sentence should say that she was relieved to *breathe* fresh air.

52. **(A)** *Pronoun Case*

People should be modified by the pronoun *who*. The pronoun *that* modifies almost everything else (such as objects and ideas). To fix the pronoun error, replace *that* with *who*: *the two friends who went to high school.*

53. **(E)** *No Error*

No error.

54. **(C)** *Comparative Modifier*

Sometimes people use the words *less* and *fewer* interchangeably, but these words have different applications. You should use *less* when you compare things that can't be counted: *she displayed less emotion than he did.* You should use fewer when you compare things that can be counted: *she ate fewer beans than he did.* Since you can count pieces of candy, use *fewer* when comparing what the sisters had: *she had gotten fewer pieces of candy than her sister.*

55. **(B)** *Tense*

The tense error in this sentence will probably sound jarring to you. The verbs *had been able* and *would have come* are in the past tense, but *will win* is in the future tense. You can fix this error by changing *will win* to the past tense: *would have won.*

56. **(D)** *Faulty Comparison*

The original sentence makes a faulty comparison between the *differing point of view* and *her.* On the SAT II Writing, you can compare points of view to other points of view, but you can't compare points of view to people. The sentence should say that Lesley opposed any point of views that differed from *hers* or from *her point of view.*

57. **(A)** *Redundancy*

In the year 1973 is a redundant expression. You don't need *the year* to explain what 1973 is. Saying *In 1973* is enough.

58. **(B)** *Pronoun Agreement*

The pronoun agreement error in this sentence is hard to spot because the pronoun comes before the noun it modifies. The subject of this sentence is the plural noun *azalea shrubs*, and it should be modified by the plural pronoun *their* instead of the singular pronoun *its.* The corrected sentence should say that *due to their hardy nature and perennial blooms, azalea shrubs have been cultivated.*

59. **(E)** *No Error*

No error.

60. **(C)** *Subject-Verb Agreement*

This sentence's compound subject, *aggressive angles and precise details*, needs to be followed by a plural verb. The first verb, *are*, is plural, but the second verb, *has been*, is singular. Correct the sentence by changing *has been* to the plural *have been.*

SAT II Writing Test 5

WRITING TEST 5 ANSWER SHEET

1. Ⓐ Ⓑ Ⓒ Ⓓ Ⓔ	21. Ⓐ Ⓑ Ⓒ Ⓓ Ⓔ	41. Ⓐ Ⓑ Ⓒ Ⓓ Ⓔ
2. Ⓐ Ⓑ Ⓒ Ⓓ Ⓔ	22. Ⓐ Ⓑ Ⓒ Ⓓ Ⓔ	42. Ⓐ Ⓑ Ⓒ Ⓓ Ⓔ
3. Ⓐ Ⓑ Ⓒ Ⓓ Ⓔ	23. Ⓐ Ⓑ Ⓒ Ⓓ Ⓔ	43. Ⓐ Ⓑ Ⓒ Ⓓ Ⓔ
4. Ⓐ Ⓑ Ⓒ Ⓓ Ⓔ	24. Ⓐ Ⓑ Ⓒ Ⓓ Ⓔ	44. Ⓐ Ⓑ Ⓒ Ⓓ Ⓔ
5. Ⓐ Ⓑ Ⓒ Ⓓ Ⓔ	25. Ⓐ Ⓑ Ⓒ Ⓓ Ⓔ	45. Ⓐ Ⓑ Ⓒ Ⓓ Ⓔ
6. Ⓐ Ⓑ Ⓒ Ⓓ Ⓔ	26. Ⓐ Ⓑ Ⓒ Ⓓ Ⓔ	46. Ⓐ Ⓑ Ⓒ Ⓓ Ⓔ
7. Ⓐ Ⓑ Ⓒ Ⓓ Ⓔ	27. Ⓐ Ⓑ Ⓒ Ⓓ Ⓔ	47. Ⓐ Ⓑ Ⓒ Ⓓ Ⓔ
8. Ⓐ Ⓑ Ⓒ Ⓓ Ⓔ	28. Ⓐ Ⓑ Ⓒ Ⓓ Ⓔ	48. Ⓐ Ⓑ Ⓒ Ⓓ Ⓔ
9. Ⓐ Ⓑ Ⓒ Ⓓ Ⓔ	29. Ⓐ Ⓑ Ⓒ Ⓓ Ⓔ	49. Ⓐ Ⓑ Ⓒ Ⓓ Ⓔ
10. Ⓐ Ⓑ Ⓒ Ⓓ Ⓔ	30. Ⓐ Ⓑ Ⓒ Ⓓ Ⓔ	50. Ⓐ Ⓑ Ⓒ Ⓓ Ⓔ
11. Ⓐ Ⓑ Ⓒ Ⓓ Ⓔ	31. Ⓐ Ⓑ Ⓒ Ⓓ Ⓔ	51. Ⓐ Ⓑ Ⓒ Ⓓ Ⓔ
12. Ⓐ Ⓑ Ⓒ Ⓓ Ⓔ	32. Ⓐ Ⓑ Ⓒ Ⓓ Ⓔ	52. Ⓐ Ⓑ Ⓒ Ⓓ Ⓔ
13. Ⓐ Ⓑ Ⓒ Ⓓ Ⓔ	33. Ⓐ Ⓑ Ⓒ Ⓓ Ⓔ	53. Ⓐ Ⓑ Ⓒ Ⓓ Ⓔ
14. Ⓐ Ⓑ Ⓒ Ⓓ Ⓔ	34. Ⓐ Ⓑ Ⓒ Ⓓ Ⓔ	54. Ⓐ Ⓑ Ⓒ Ⓓ Ⓔ
15. Ⓐ Ⓑ Ⓒ Ⓓ Ⓔ	35. Ⓐ Ⓑ Ⓒ Ⓓ Ⓔ	55. Ⓐ Ⓑ Ⓒ Ⓓ Ⓔ
16. Ⓐ Ⓑ Ⓒ Ⓓ Ⓔ	36. Ⓐ Ⓑ Ⓒ Ⓓ Ⓔ	56. Ⓐ Ⓑ Ⓒ Ⓓ Ⓔ
17. Ⓐ Ⓑ Ⓒ Ⓓ Ⓔ	37. Ⓐ Ⓑ Ⓒ Ⓓ Ⓔ	57. Ⓐ Ⓑ Ⓒ Ⓓ Ⓔ
18. Ⓐ Ⓑ Ⓒ Ⓓ Ⓔ	38. Ⓐ Ⓑ Ⓒ Ⓓ Ⓔ	58. Ⓐ Ⓑ Ⓒ Ⓓ Ⓔ
19. Ⓐ Ⓑ Ⓒ Ⓓ Ⓔ	39. Ⓐ Ⓑ Ⓒ Ⓓ Ⓔ	59. Ⓐ Ⓑ Ⓒ Ⓓ Ⓔ
20. Ⓐ Ⓑ Ⓒ Ⓓ Ⓔ	40. Ⓐ Ⓑ Ⓒ Ⓓ Ⓔ	60. Ⓐ Ⓑ Ⓒ Ⓓ Ⓔ

WRITING TEST 5

You have twenty minutes to plan and write an essay on the topic assigned below. DO NOT WRITE ON ANOTHER TOPIC. AN ESSAY ON ANOTHER TOPIC IS NOT ACCEPTABLE.

The essay is assigned to give you an opportunity to show how well you can write. You should, therefore, take care to express your thoughts on the topic clearly and effectively. How well you write is much more important than how much you write, but to cover the topic adequately you will probably need to write more than one paragraph. Be specific.

Your essay must be written on the following two pages. You will find that you have enough space if you write on every line, avoid wide margins, and keep your handwriting to a reasonable size. It is important to remember that what you write will be read by someone who is not familiar with your handwriting. Try to write or print so that what you are writing is legible to the reader.

Consider the following statements and assignment. Then write the essay as directed.

"Knowledge is power."
"Ignorance is bliss."

Assignment: Choose one example from personal experience, current events, or history, literature, or any other discipline and use this example to write an essay in which you agree or disagree with only one of the two statements above. Your essay should be specific.

DO NOT WRITE YOUR ESSAY IN YOUR TEST BOOK. You will receive credit only for what you write on your answer sheet.

WHEN YOUR SUPERVISOR ANNOUNCES THAT TWENTY MINUTES HAVE PASSED, YOU MUST STOP WRITING THE ESSAY AND GO ON TO PART B IF YOU HAVE NOT ALREADY DONE SO. IF YOU FINISH YOUR ESSAY BEFORE THIS ANNOUNCEMENT, GO ON TO PART B AT ONCE.

BEGIN WRITING YOUR ESSAY ON THE ANSWER SHEET.

WRITING TEST

Part A

Time — 20 minutes

WRITING TEST

Part A

Time — 20 minutes

WRITING TEST

Part B

Time — 40 minutes

<u>Directions:</u> The following sentences test your knowledge of grammar, usage, diction (choice of words), and idiom.

Some sentences are correct.
No sentence contains more than one error.

You will find that the error, if there is one, is underlined and lettered. Elements of the sentence that are not underlined will not be changed. In choosing answers, follow the requirements of standard written English.

If there is an error, select the <u>one underlined part</u> that must be changed to make the sentence correct and fill in the corresponding oval on your answer sheet.

If there is no answer, fill in answer oval Ⓔ.

EXAMPLE:

SAMPLE ANSWER:

<u>The other</u> delegates and <u>him</u> <u>immediately</u>
   A   B   C

accepted the resolution <u>drafted by</u> the
                      D

neutral states. <u>No error</u>
              E

Ⓐ ● Ⓒ Ⓓ Ⓔ

---

1. <u>Many</u> consumers objected to the misleading manner <u>in</u>
  A   B

which the company diverted attention from <u>their</u>
                                   C

<u>recently</u> raised prices. <u>No error</u>
  D   E

2. After the meteorologists announced <u>that</u> there would
                            A

be <u>record-breaking</u> coastal floods the next day, the
    B

vacationers tried to get out of the town as <u>quick</u> <u>as</u>
                                C   D

possible. <u>No error</u>
      E

3. When Jessica said that she <u>wanted to go</u> to a midnight
                           A

screening <u>of</u> *The Rocky Horror Picture Show*, her
       B

parents refused to allow her <u>to drive</u> into town <u>at such a</u>
                          C   D

late hour. <u>No error</u>
       E

4. Will's grandfather decreed that abiding <u>with</u> the rules
                               A

<u>of</u> the house included <u>doing</u> all of the shopping,
B   C

cooking, <u>and</u> cleaning. <u>No error</u>
       D   E

GO ON TO THE NEXT PAGE →

5. If the crew of the sailboat <u>had</u> known about the storm

                               A

   in the east, <u>it</u> <u>would have</u> redirected its course <u>to</u> the

             B   C   D

   west. <u>No error</u>

            E

6. The band, <u>which</u> was always surrounded by an

            A

   entourage of publicists and fans, <u>was</u> notorious for

                                           B

   <u>their</u> past high jinks while <u>on tour</u>. <u>No error</u>

   C   D   E

7. The group of plastic casts <u>were</u> used <u>to record</u> the

                           A   B

   <u>shape of</u> the shark's jaw before the reproduction <u>was</u>

   C   D

   built. <u>No error</u>

             E

8. Verdi's first major operatic success was <u>followed by</u> a

                                         A

   period of sustained activity <u>that</u> resulted in a series of

                          B

   operas, many of <u>whom</u> became <u>enormously</u> popular.

                  C   D

   <u>No error</u>

      E

9. A <u>naturally occurring</u> substance in tomatoes, called

        A

   lycopene <u>has been found to have</u> a beneficial effect on a

                  B

   <u>variety of</u> ailments, <u>including</u> certain cancers.

   C   D

   <u>No error</u>

      E

10. <u>Answering</u> the judge's question, the defendant stated

     A

   that his dash through the park <u>had not been</u> an

                           B

   attempt to <u>allude</u> the police <u>but</u> an attempt to catch his

           C   D

   bus. <u>No error</u>

        E

11. The first year of college is a time <u>where</u> you meet <u>many</u>

                               A   B

   of the people <u>who will become</u> your <u>lifelong</u> friends.

               C   D

   <u>No error</u>

      E

12. <u>Possessed of</u> a penetrating intellect, Bayard Rustin was

     A

   <u>as significant a figure</u> <u>than</u> any <u>other</u> in the civil rights

            B   C   D

   movement. <u>No error</u>

               E

13. <u>Although</u> less famous than her <u>siblings</u>, Anne Bronte's

     A   B

   novel <u>was</u> purchased and published in the late

          C

   nineteenth century <u>by</u> a reputable British press.

                  D

   <u>No error</u>

      E

14. Over the past ten years, <u>while training</u> in Vienna, she

                         A

   <u>will have</u> <u>achieved</u> great success, winning some of the

     B   C

   <u>most</u> prestigious prizes for young opera singers. <u>No error</u>

   D   E

15. No one among the explorers <u>was</u> more disappointed

                          A

   than <u>him</u> when heavy rains in the region <u>delayed</u> the

       B   C

   expedition <u>by</u> a month. <u>No error</u>

          D   E

16. <u>Having</u> reviewed the research, the examiners

     A

   <u>concluded</u> that <u>neither</u> of the scientist's proofs <u>were</u>

     B   C   D

   valid. <u>No error</u>

         E

GO ON TO THE NEXT PAGE

17. <u>After spending</u> all day <u>indoors</u>, Mary and Bob decided
　　　　A　　　　　　　　　　B

　　to put on their <u>coat</u> and get some fresh air <u>at</u> the park.
　　　　　　　　　C　　　　　　　　　　　　　D

　　<u>No error</u>
　　　E

18. She agreed to go on the hiking trip <u>without realizing</u>
　　　　　　　　　　　　　　　　　　　A

　　that she would be walking <u>all day long</u>, living <u>out of</u> a
　　　　　　　　　　　　　　　B　　　　　　　C

　　backpack, and <u>have to eat</u> nothing but canned fish.
　　　　　　　　　D

　　<u>No error</u>
　　　E

19. When she heard that she <u>had lost</u> the election for class
　　　　　　　　　　　　　　　　A

　　president, she began <u>to argue</u> <u>against</u> the principal
　　　　　　　　　　　　　B　　　　C

　　about the accuracy <u>of</u> the ballot count. <u>No error</u>
　　　　　　　　　　D　　　　　　　　　　E

20. Only after the boy had <u>tore</u> down the opposing <u>team's</u>
　　　　　　　　　　　　　A　　　　　　　　　　B

　　banners <u>did</u> he realize <u>how</u> unsportsmanlike his
　　　　　C　　　　　　　D

　　actions had been. <u>No error</u>
　　　　　　　　　E

GO ON TO THE NEXT PAGE

WRITING TEST

21. One of the functions of the Hubble Space Telescope is to locate and photographing the birth of stars.

    (A) is to locate and photographing the birth of stars
    (B) is to locate and having photographed the births of stars
    (C) is locating and photographing the birth of stars
    (D) are to locate and photographing the birth of a star
    (E) are locating and also photographing star births

22. The new conservation equipment enabled the museum to restore the damaged painting and it was also able to fix the chip on the sculpture by Bernini.

    (A) and it was also able to fix
    (B) as well as fixing
    (C) and to fix
    (D) and also fixing
    (E) so it could fix

23. The construction of a new gym had been supported by the school board until it was realized by the superintendent that the school didn't have enough funds to complete the project.

    (A) The construction of a new gym had been supported by the school board until it was realized by the superintendent that the school didn't have enough funds to complete the project.
    (B) The construction of a new gym was being supported by the school board until it was realized by the superintendent that the school didn't have enough funds to complete the project.
    (C) The construction of a new gym had been supported by the school board until the superintendent had realized that the school didn't have enough funds to complete the project.
    (D) The school board had supported the construction of a new gym until it was realized by the superintendent that the school didn't have enough funds to complete the project.
    (E) The school board had supported the construction of a new gym until the superintendent realized that the school didn't have enough funds to complete the project.

GO ON TO THE NEXT PAGE →

24. Many people experience memory loss, poor concentration, and <u>are unable to control their impulses when they are deprived</u> of sleep.

    (A) are unable to control their impulses when they are deprived
    (B) are unable to control their impulses when deprived
    (C) an inability to control their impulses when they are deprived
    (D) an inability to control his or her impulses when they are deprived
    (E) an inability of controlling their impulses when deprived

25. Seats are still available <u>on the afternoon train you can purchase your ticket at the station</u>.

    (A) on the afternoon train you can purchase your ticket at the station
    (B) on the afternoon train; you can purchase your ticket at the station
    (C) at the station on the afternoon train, you can purchase your ticktet
    (D) on the afternoon train and at the station, where you can purchase your ticket
    (E) on the afternoon train, and at the station is where you can purchase your ticket

26. After the media vilified him, <u>booing and jeering the man</u> wherever he went.

    (A) booing and jeering the man
    (B) and yet they were booing and jeering the man
    (C) but the man was booed and also jeered
    (D) the man was booed and jeered
    (E) additionally the booed and jeered man

27. Like many neophytes in the business world, <u>the discovery of the depths to which his rivals would stoop in order to maintain their share of the market shocked him</u>.

    (A) the discovery of the depths to which his rivals would stoop in order to maintain their share of the market shocked him
    (B) the discovery of the depths to which his rivals would stoop in order to maintain his or her share of the market shocked him
    (C) he was shocked to discover the depths to which his rivals would stoop in order to maintain their share of the market.
    (D) he was shocked to discover the depths to which his rivals would stoop in order to maintain his or her share of the market.
    (E) he was shocked to discover his rivals stooping to such depths to have maintained their share of the market.

28. <u>An electronic device that allows a deaf person to hear, a hearing aid consists of a miniature sound receiver, an amplifier, and to transfer the amplified sound by either an earpiece or a vibrator.</u>

    (A) An electronic device that allows a deaf person to hear, a hearing aid consists of a miniature sound receiver, an amplifier, and to transfer the amplified sound by either an earpiece or a vibrator.
    (B) An electronic device that allows a deaf person to hear, a hearing aid consists of a miniature sound receiver, an amplifier, and either an earpiece or a vibrator to transfer the amplified sound.
    (C) An electronic device that allows a deaf person to hear, consisting of a miniature sound receiver, an amplifier, and either an earpiece or a vibrator, making for a hearing aid.
    (D) Allowing a deaf person to hear electronically, a hearing aid, which will consist of a miniature sound receiver, an amplifier, and an earpiece or a vibrator.
    (E) Consisting of a miniature sound receiver, an amplifier, and either an earpiece or a vibrator to transfer the amplified sound, a deaf person can hear with such an aid.

GO ON TO THE NEXT PAGE

29. A rhetorical question has several uses: <u>it can be used for emphasis as well as for sarcasm and for style as well as for content</u>.

   (A) it can be used for emphasis as well as for sarcasm and for style as well as for content
   (B) they can be used for emphasis as well as for sarcasm or for style or content
   (C) it can be useful when it comes to emphasis, sarcasm, style, or content
   (D) because it can be used for emphasis as well as for sarcasm or it can be used for style as well as for content
   (E) because they can be used for emphasis as well as for sarcasm or they can be used for style as well as for content

30. In order to have had the opportunity to advance to the next level, the students <u>will have to get</u> serious about their work very early in the semester.

   (A) will have to get
   (B) would have had to have gotten
   (C) would have had to have been getting to be
   (D) will have to be getting
   (E) will have had to have been

31. None of the chief executives of retiring age <u>were willing to accept the incentive package offered by the foundering company</u>.

   (A) were willing to accept the incentive package offered by the foundering company
   (B) were willing to accept the foundering company's incentive package
   (C) were willing to accept the foundering company's incentive package that was being offered
   (D) was willing to accept the offering, by the foundering company, of the incentive package
   (E) was willing to accept the incentive package offered by the foundering company

32. Some people point to the advantages of a job offering security <u>over a job offering creative fulfillment</u>.

   (A) over a job offering creative fulfillment
   (B) over a job which will offer creative fulfillment
   (C) over the advantages of a job offering creative fulfillment
   (D) instead of the advantages of a job which offered creative fulfillment
   (E) instead of a job which offers creative fulfillment

33. Neither the groom's sister nor the bride's brothers <u>was planning to attend the wedding, which the siblings disapproved of</u>.

   (A) was planning to attend the wedding, which the siblings disapproved of
   (B) was planning to attend the wedding, of which the siblings disapproved
   (C) were planning to attend the wedding, which the siblings were disapproving of
   (D) were planning to attend the wedding, of which the siblings disapproved
   (E) were planning to attend the wedding, and the siblings disapproved of it

34. Some people consider *Duck Soup* to be the best Marx Brothers <u>movie; at the time of its release, however,</u> it was not very popular with critics or audiences.

   (A) movie; at the time of its release, however,
   (B) movie, but at the time of its release, however,
   (C) movie, however, having been released at the time,
   (D) movie, having been released,
   (E) movie: however, released at the time,

35. Evelyn Waugh wrote <u>novels and they satirize</u> upper-class English society in the 1920s and 1930s.

   (A) novels and they satirize
   (B) novels, being satires of
   (C) novels, they satirize
   (D) novels that satirize
   (E) novels, and satirizing in them

36. <u>The belief that the earth was the center of the universe prevailed until the seventeenth century.</u>

   (A) The belief that the earth was the center of the universe prevailed until the seventeenth century.
   (B) The belief that prevailed about the earth being the center of the universe was until the seventeenth century.
   (C) Until the seventeenth century, they had a prevailing belief in the fact that the earth was the center of the universe.
   (D) Prevalent as a belief until the seventeenth century was that the earth was the center of the universe.
   (E) Believing that the earth was the center of the universe prevailed until the seventeenth century.

GO ON TO THE NEXT PAGE

37. <u>Olivia was relieved to find the flute she had been searching for walking by the kitchen table.</u>

    (A) Olivia was relieved to find the flute she had been searching for walking by the kitchen table.
    (B) Olivia was relieved when she found the flute, walking by the kitchen table, which she had been searching for.
    (C) Walking by the kitchen table, Olivia was relieved to find the flute she had been searching for.
    (D) Relieved to find the flute she had been searching for, Olivia was walking by the kitchen table.
    (E) Relieved, the flute that Olivia had been searching for was found walking by the kitchen table.

38. <u>Rejected by several magazines, an early story by J.D. Salinger eventually</u> developed into *The Catcher in the Rye*.

    (A) Rejected by several magazines, an early story by J.D. Salinger eventually
    (B) Rejecting several magazines, J.D. Salinger's early story
    (C) Eventually rejected by several magazines, J.D. Salinger wrote an early story which
    (D) J.D. Salinger, who was rejected by several magazines, eventually wrote an early story
    (E) Being rejected by several magazines, an early story by J.D. Salinger eventually

GO ON TO THE NEXT PAGE

WRITING TEST

Directions: Each of the following passages is an early draft of an essay. Some parts of the passages need to be rewritten.

Read each passage and answer the questions that follow. Some questions are about particular sentences or parts of sentences and ask you to improve sentence structure and word choice. Other questions refer to parts of the essay or the entire essay and ask you to consider organization and development. In making your decisions, follow the conventions of standard written English. After you have chosen your answer, fill in the corresponding oval on your answer sheet.

Questions 39–44 are based on the following passage.

(1) *Baseball is truly America's pastime.* (2) *Even though some people think that it's boring, however I think it is the most enjoyable of all the spectator sports.* (3) *There's no better way to spend a sunny, summer afternoon than at the ballpark, where there is plenty of excitement both on and off the field.*

(4) *Some of my friends say that baseball is boring.* (5) *The game seems slow.* (6) *The leisurely pace of the game is partly what makes it great.* (7) *(Why does everything in modern life have to happen really quick anyway?)* (8) *My friends may think baseball has a lot of dead time, but there's always something going on, and it's not always on the field.* (9) *For example, if you think everything seems dead on the field, one should look at the dugouts because the teams' managers will probably be signaling to its players.*

(10) *The ballparks organize many entertaining events to amuse the crowds.* (11) *Once I was chosen to go out on the field, and I had three chances to throw a strike.* (12) *I didn't succeed.* (13) *I was still given a signed baseball.* (14) *That's why I think baseball is awesome.*

39. Which of the following is the best version of sentence 2 (reproduced below)?

Even though some people think it's boring, however I think it is the most enjoyable of all the spectator sports.

(A) (As it is now)
(B) Even though some people think its boring, however, I think its the most enjoyable of all the spectator sports.
(C) Even though some people think it's boring; however, I think it is the more enjoyable spectator sport.
(D) Even though some people think it's boring, I think it is the most enjoyable spectator sport.
(E) However some people think it's boring, I think it is the most enjoyable of all of the spectator sports.

40. Which of the following is the best way to combine sentences 4 and 5 (reproduced below)?

Some of my friends say that baseball is boring. The game seems slow.

(A) Some of my friends say that baseball is boring because the game seems slow.
(B) Some of my friends say that baseball is boring; the game seems slow.
(C) Some of my friends say that baseball is boring, but the game seems slow.
(D) Some of my friends say that baseball is boring; despite this, the game seems slow.
(E) Some of my friends say that baseball is boring, the game seems slow.

GO ON TO THE NEXT PAGE ➡

41. In the context of the second paragraph, which of the following would be the most suitable phrase to insert at the beginning of sentence 6 ?

    (A) Subsequently,
    (B) In my opinion,
    (C) By contrast,
    (D) Disagreeing with what they say,
    (E) In addition,

42. Which of the following is the best revision of the underlined portion of sentence 9 (reproduced below)?

    For example, if you think everything seems dead on the field, <u>one should look at the dugouts because the teams' managers will probably be signaling to its players</u>.

    (A) (As it is now)
    (B) one should look at the dugouts because the managers of the teams will probably be signaling to its players
    (C) one should look at the dugouts because the teams' managers will probably have been signaling to their players
    (D) you should look at the dugouts because the teams' managers will probably be signaling to their players
    (E) you should look to the dugouts because the teams' managers will probably be signaling by its players

43. Which of the following sentences is best inserted before sentence 10, at the beginning of the third paragraph?

    (A) Now I'll tell you about one time when I was the one being signaled to.
    (B) Baseball offers many other diversions that have nothing to do with the game.
    (C) It is obvious that baseball is not boring.
    (D) Baseball managers all use different kinds of signals.
    (E) There is something else that is fun about baseball, but it is not always involving the game itself.

44. The writer uses all of the following techniques EXCEPT:

    (A) presenting an argument
    (B) giving an opposing viewpoint
    (C) debunking a popular belief
    (D) describing a hypothetical situation
    (E) telling a personal story

GO ON TO THE NEXT PAGE

Questions 45–50 are based on the following passage.

(1) Perception is a tricky issue; how people perceive things can differ in surprising ways. (2) Many people probably believe that there's an objective truth to events and things, even if it is not always obvious. (3) I don't see how we could ever know this truth, since everyone knows only their subjective viewpoints. (4) How can we know whether what I perceive to be the color red is the same as what you perceive to be red? (5) My guess is that we'll never know the answer to this.

(6) The issue of perception began to bother me recently when I saw a new television show. (7) The show tells the same story (usually about a murder) from the viewpoints of the people involved in the crime. (8) Watching this show, the realization that people view the same events in many different ways dawned on me.

(9) I remembered a book that I read called World's End by T. C. Boyle. (10) In this book, the protagonist loses both of his feet. (11) He imagined he can still feel them. (12) I heard that amputees often sense in their missing limbs physical sensations and are convinced that they are still there. (13) This phenomenon also seems to be an issue of perception, since the limbs are clearly gone, but the people still feel them.

45. Which of the following is the best revision of the underlined part of sentence 3 (reproduced below)?

   I don't see how we could ever know this truth, since <u>everyone knows only their subjective viewpoints</u>.

   (A) everyone had known their subjective viewpoints
   (B) everyone know only their subjective viewpoints
   (C) only everyone knows their subjective viewpoints
   (D) everyone know only his or her viewpoint
   (E) everyone knows only his or her viewpoint

46. Sentence 4 serves as

   (A) the argument of the essay
   (B) an example of the problem of subjectivity
   (C) the question the essay tries to answer
   (D) a personal anecdote
   (E) the conclusion of the essay

47. In context, inserting which of the following words after "*this*" would make sentence 5 more precise?

   (A) color
   (B) viewpoint
   (C) question
   (D) issue of perception
   (E) truth

48. Which of the following is the best revision of sentence 8 (reproduced below)?

   Watching this show, the realization that people view the same events in many different ways dawned on me.

   (A) (As it is now)
   (B) Having watched this show, the realization that people viewed the same events in many different ways has dawned on me.
   (C) Watching this show, the realization of viewing the same events in many different ways dawned on me.
   (D) Watching this show, I realized the fact that the same events can be viewed in many different ways by people.
   (E) Watching this show, I realized that people view the same events in many different ways.

GO ON TO THE NEXT PAGE

49. Which of the following is the best revision and combination of sentences 10 and 11 (reproduced below)?

    In this book, the protagonist loses both of his feet. He imagined that he can still feel them.

    (A) In this book, despite the fact that he loses both of his feet, the protagonist imagined that he can still feel them.
    (B) In this book, the protagonist loses both of his feet, but he imagines that he can still feel them.
    (C) The protagonist who is in this book loses both of his feet, and he imagines that he could still feel them.
    (D) Although the protagonist loses both of his feet, in this book he imagined that he can still feel the feet.
    (E) Losing both of his feet in the book, the protagonist imagines he can still feel them.

50. Which of the following is the best replacement for "*they*" in sentence 12 ?

    (A) (As it is now)
    (B) these limbs
    (C) they themselves
    (D) the amputees
    (E) these sensations

GO ON TO THE NEXT PAGE

WRITING TEST

51. Benedict strained to hear the people in the room
              A

    next door, but because the walls were thick, their
                        B   C

    conversation was unintelligent. No error
                 D   E

52. Although the horse jumped the fences as graceful as
                                 A

    she could, she never stood a chance against the more
     B   C   D

    seasoned competitors. No error
              E

53. Because there was not scarcely any snow falling when
   A   B

    it left, the family neglected to pack the snowshoes it
  C

    would need to navigate the deep drifts. No error
    D   E

54. Protesters were understandably upset when they
           A   B

    wrote that only ten thousand demonstrators had
       C   D

    attended the rally. No error
         E

55. Admitting that her previous assignment to learn forty
    A   B

    words each night may have been unrealistic, the
                  C

    teacher modified the next homework assignment.
       D

    No error
  E

56. The team of pediatric surgeons was delighted to learn
                    A   B

    that their efforts had been honored with a prestigious
    C

    award and much acclaim. No error
        D   E

57. In accordance in its laws, Britain declined to prosecute
         A   B

    the offender, choosing instead to deport him the
         C

    following morning. No error
   D   E

GO ON TO THE NEXT PAGE →

58. The prosecuting attorney complained privately <u>to</u> the
                                                  A

    judge that <u>the defense's argument</u> relied on
                        B

    the testimony of a witness who was <u>hardly</u> <u>credulous</u>.
                                          C   D

    <u>No error</u>
        E

59. The girl <u>complained</u> that if there had been <u>less</u>
                  A   B

    distractions in the classroom, she <u>would have been able</u>
                                            C

    to concentrate <u>on taking</u> the test. <u>No error</u>
                       D   E

60. Matthew was interested <u>in buying</u> the car that had
                               A

    been advertised in the Sunday newspaper, <u>but</u> when
                                                 B

    he called the owner, he was disappointed <u>to learn</u> that
                                                 C

    it <u>had already been sold</u>. <u>No error</u>
           D   E

S T O P

IF YOU FINISH BEFORE TIME IS CALLED, YOU MAY CHECK YOUR WORK ON THIS TEST ONLY.
DO NOT TURN TO ANY OTHER TEST IN THIS BOOK.

SAT II Writing Practice Test 5 Explanations

Calculating Your Score

Question Number	Correct Answer	Right	Wrong	Question Number	Correct Answer	Right	Wrong
1.	C	___	___	31.	E	___	___
2.	C	___	___	32.	C	___	___
3.	E	___	___	33.	D	___	___
4.	A	___	___	34.	A	___	___
5.	E	___	___	35.	D	___	___
6.	C	___	___	36.	A	___	___
7.	A	___	___	37.	C	___	___
8.	C	___	___	38.	A	___	___
9.	E	___	___	39.	D	___	___
10.	C	___	___	40.	A	___	___
11.	A	___	___	41.	B	___	___
12.	C	___	___	42.	D	___	___
13.	B	___	___	43.	B	___	___
14.	B	___	___	44.	C	___	___
15.	B	___	___	45.	E	___	___
16.	D	___	___	46.	B	___	___
17.	D	___	___	47.	C	___	___
18.	D	___	___	48.	E	___	___
19.	C	___	___	49.	B	___	___
20.	A	___	___	50.	B	___	___
21.	C	___	___	51.	D	___	___
22.	C	___	___	52.	A	___	___
23.	E	___	___	53.	B	___	___
24.	C	___	___	54.	B	___	___
25.	B	___	___	55.	E	___	___
26.	D	___	___	56.	C	___	___
27.	C	___	___	57.	A	___	___
28.	B	___	___	58.	D	___	___
29.	A	___	___	59.	B	___	___
30.	B	___	___	60.	E	___	___

Your raw score for the SAT II Writing test is a composite of your raw score in the multiple-choice section and your score on the essay. Once you have determined your composite score, use the conversion table on pages 16-17 to calculate your scaled score. To calculate your raw score, count the number of questions you answered correctly on the multiple choice: _____ A

Count the number of questions you answered incorrectly, and multiply that number by $\frac{1}{4}$:

_____ B $\times \frac{1}{4} =$ _____ C

Subtract the value in field C from value in field A: _____ D

Round the number to the nearest whole number: _____ E

Take your score for the essay (ask a teacher to grade your essay or grade yourself) and multiply it by 3.43:

_____ F $\times 3.43 =$ _____ G

Add the number in field E to the number in Field G: _____ H

Round the number in field H. This is your SAT II Writing score: _____

Test 5 Explanations

Student Essays

Total Score: 12 (each reader gave the essay a 6)

The African-American experience proves that knowledge—both book-knowledge and self-knowledge—is power. Maybe not power in the conventional sense of having control over other people, but definitely in the sense of not being subject to others' control and of having dignity and pride in oneself. In his autobiographical Narrative, *Frederick Douglass describes how knowledge gave him the power to resist slavery. In the twentieth-century novel* A Lesson Before Dying, *the two African-American protagonists develop self-knowledge and free themselves emotionally from the oppresive white society.*

In his autobiography, Frederick Douglass explains how knowledge showed him the path to freedom. When Douglass is seven or eight years old, his mistress in Baltimore teaches him the alphabet. He realizes the power of education when he overhears his master reprimanding his wife, saying that education ruins slaves and makes them unmanageable. This is a pivotal moment in Douglass's life because he realizes that education is the difference between slaves and white men and resolves to teach himself reading and writing. When he returns to plantation life, he suffers through some hard years of labor. At times, he feels like the sheer brutality of his existence will overwhelm him, but he regains his dignity when he fights with one of the particularly cruel masters. Eventually he escapes to freedom in the North. Douglass's education helps him realize his humanity and the injustice of his situation. It keeps him from submitting emotionally, as well as physically, to slavery and from giving up in despair. His education did not directly give him freedom, but it did give him knowledge of his self-worth.

In A Lesson Before Dying, *Ernest Gaines writes about the oppressive society in the 1940s South. The plot centers on Jefferson, an African-American man who has been sentenced to death. During the trial, Jefferson's white lawyer defends him by saying that Jefferson is too dumb to have committed the crime and compared him to a hog. Hoping to help Jefferson die like a man instead of an animal, Jefferson's godmother and her friend enlist the help of Grant, an educated African-American man with mixed feelings about his community. By befriending him, Grant helps Jefferson develop a sense of self-worth and dignity. Jefferson learns that he is a man, not a hog, and that his actions will influence others in his community. With this restored humanity, Jefferson faces his execution bravely, defying white stereotypes that compare African Americans to animals. Like Jefferson, Grant also learns from their friendship; he developes pride in his actions and learns to face difficulties head-on.*

The kind of knowledge Jefferson acquires is not from books, but from friendship, love, and pride. In both of these books, self-knowledge plays an important role because it teaches the protagonists about their humanity. Their self-awareness prevents other people from trampling on their minds and spirits, even when people degrade them physically.

Discussion:

This essay responds to the statement that "knowledge is power" using a coherent argument, interesting examples, and fairly clear prose. Although the essay has a few flaws, overall it shows competence, earning it a combined score of 12.

The writer argues that two African-American experiences, one real and one fictional, attest to the truth of the statement. The argument benefits from the similarities between the examples. Both of them deal with the oppression of African Americans, and both of them illustrate how African Americans are able to overcome enslavement and racism by realizing their dignity and humanity.

Instead of limiting the definition of knowledge to what is taught in schools and the definition of power to control, the writer has a less strict, but ultimately more interesting, take on the words. According to the writer, one form of knowledge is self-knowledge, and one form of power is the ability to resist external influence, particularly when it is hard to resist. The writer could improve the essay by clearly defining his use of these words.

The introduction is the weakest part of the essay. The argument is confined to one short sentence, and the transitions between the sentences feel abrupt. The introduction also contains the biggest grammatical error in the essay: the second sentence is a fragment, not a complete sentence.

The second and third paragraphs on *The Narrative of the Life of Frederick Douglass* and Gaines's *A Lesson Before Dying* are quite well-developed. In the second paragraph, the writer explains how Douglass's education teaches him that the differences between slaves and their masters are artificial. This knowledge gives him the strength to overcome slavery's degrading effects. The example from *A Lesson Before Dying* is less clear than the Douglass example. The writer's description of the knowledge that Jefferson and Grant acquire is a little sketchy, and the last line feels a little tagged on, as if the writer suddenly remembered to include a sentence about Grant's acquired knowledge.

At times the sentences sound a little choppy in the second and third paragraphs, but overall the writing is clear and correct. The major grammatical error in this section occurs at the start of the third paragraph, where the writer makes a tense error: *Jefferson's white lawyer defends him by saying that Jefferson is too dumb to have committed the crime and compared him to a hog.* Since the action in the sentence takes place in the present tense, the writer should replace *compared* with *compares*.

The conclusion to this essay is strong because it doesn't repeat what the author wrote in the introduction; instead, it expands on the similarities between the two stories.

Total Score: 4 (each reader gave the essay a 2)

I think there is alot to be said about "ignorance is bliss." This statement is really true in some cases, even if it isn't true in others. But in this essay I will talk about the times when the statement is true. Such as when knowing something can hurt your feelings or make someone responsible for things they don't want to be responsible for.

One time that I wish I didn't know things was when my friends were talking behind my back. I didn't know it at the time, of course. I found out later, I was really hurt. They said I was "lame" and tried to hard to fit in. Maybe that was true, but I just wanted them to like me. One day I saw them laughing at me, I ran away crying. There not my friends now. I wish I had never been friends with them.

Another example of ignorance is bliss is from a book I read in class. In this book, called The Picture of Dorian Gray, *by Wilde, the handsum man Dorian Gray has bliss while he doesn't know that beauty doesn't last. When Dorian meets a guy who tells him that he will get old and ugly, Dorian curses a picture of himself, says that the picture should get old while Dorian stays young and beautiful. He starts to turn into a really bad guy. He was much sweeter and nicer before he knew about old age. The strange thing is that the painting starts to get really ugly as Dorian gets ugly in his heart. But Dorian's real looks don't change (I think, until the end). In sum, his caractor is much nicer before he loses his ignorance.*

Discussion:

This essay gets a combined score of 4 because it demonstrates "some incompetence." The writer uses one bad example and one undeveloped example to back up the weak argument, and the writing is riddled with grammatical and spelling errors.

The essay gets off to a poor start. Since the essay is supposed to express the writer's personal views, there is no need to use phrases like *I think* or *in my opinion*. There is also no need to write that there is a lot (not *alot*) to be said about "ignorance is bliss." Of course there's a lot to say about the subject; that's why the writer chose to write the essay.

The writer could improve the introduction by stating the argument in more definitive terms than *but in this essay I will talk about the times when the statement is true*. The introduction should also introduce the examples the writer will use to support the argument: in this case, the malicious friends and the corrupted Dorian Gray. Instead, the writer discusses vague, hypothetical situations. To make matters worse, the last sentence of the introduction is a sentence fragment.

You should be cautious when using personal examples in your essay. This writer makes an unwise decision to talk about the deceitful friends. As a general rule, personal examples should try to cast you in a positive light, but this examples makes the writer seem unliked and a little pathetic. Another problem with this example is that it doesn't really address "ignorance is bliss." Instead, it suggests that knowledge can be hurtful. If the writer plans to use this example, then the link between ignorance and bliss must be made explicit.

The second paragraph contains several technical errors. The writer makes two run-on sentences: *I found out later, I was really hurt* and *One day I saw them laughing at me, I ran away crying.* The paragraph also has some spelling mistakes: *to* instead of *too* and *there* instead of *they're*.

The topic of the third paragraph is probably the best aspect of this essay, although the writer fails to develop the example well. The writer talks about how Dorian Gray's realization that beauty is transient ultimately leads him down a corrupt path, but the writer does not explain how or why this change happens. The writer should also provide some more details about Dorian's happy existence before he realizes the truth about his looks and about his transformation into a corrupt man. Fleshing out this example could really boost the essay's score, especially since it is an unusual and potentially interesting book to write about.

The third paragraph also contains spelling and structural problems. The writer misspells *handsome* as *handsum* and *character* as *caractor*, and the tone in this paragraph is inappropriately slangy (the writer should call Dorian a *man* instead of a *guy*, for instance).

Another major flaw with this essay is its lack of a conclusion. Even if short on time, the writer should have tried to put down at least one concluding sentence.

Identifying Sentence Errors

1. **(C)**   *Pronoun Agreement*

The sentence makes a pronoun agreement error when it says *their recently raised prices. Their*, a plural pronoun, stands in for *company's*, as in *the company's recently raised prices*. Since *company* is a singular noun, the pronoun preceding *recently raised prices* should also be singular. In order to fix this agreement error, you need to change the plural pronoun *their* to the singular pronoun *its*.

2. **(C)**   *Adverb*

Verbs should be modified by adverbs, and nouns should be modified by adjectives. In this sentence, the adjective *quick* incorrectly modifies the verb *to get out*. You need to change *quick* to the adverb *quickly*, so the sentence says that *the vacationers tried to get out of the town as quickly as possible*.

3. **(E)**   *No Error*

No error.

4. **(A)**   *Idiom*

You can usually catch idiom mistakes with your ear because they sound funny or unfamiliar. In this case, *abide with* is an idiomatic error. The correct expression in English is *abide by*, as in, *abiding by the rules of the house*.

5. **(E)**   *No Error*

No error.

6. **(C)**   *Pronoun Agreement*

The subject of this sentence is a singular noun: *the band*. When the sentence talks about the band's high jinks, though, it modifies the band with a plural pronoun, *their*. Since *the band* is a singular noun, the pronoun that modifies it must also be singular: *its*.

7. **(A)**   *Subject-Verb Agreement*

The subject of this sentence is the singular noun *the group*, so the verb that follows it must be the singular *was* instead of the plural *were*. Subject-verb agreement errors can be hard to spot when there's a prepositional phrase such as *of the plaster models and plastic casts* between the subject and verb of the sentence.

8. **(C)**   *Pronoun*

Whom modifies people only. *Which* modifies operas, objects, and other nonhuman things. To fix this error, replace *whom* with *which* so the sentence reads, *a series of operas, many of which became enormously popular*.

9. **(E)**   *No Error*

No error.

10. **(C)**   *Wrong Word*

Allude is the wrong word in this sentence. *To allude* means to refer to something, but the sentence wants to say that the the defendant's dash was not an attempt to *escape* the police. *To elude*, which means to escape or avoid detection, is the correct word in this context.

11. **(A)**   *Idiom*

Where primarily describes location. It should not modify *a time*, as it does in this sentence. To fix the sentence, you should subsitute *when* for *where*, since *when* describes time.

12. **(C)**   *Idiom*

When the sentence says that Rustin was *as significant a figure than any other*, it makes an idiomatic error. The correct idiom is *as something as something else*. Change *than* to *as* to fix this error: Rustin *was as significant a figure as any other*. The phrase *possessed of* may sound funny to you, but the expression is correct. Saying that Rustin is *possessed of* a penetrating intellect is the same as saying that he *has* a penetrating intellect.

13. **(B)**   *Faulty Comparison*

The sentence says that *Anne Bronte's novel* was less famous than *her siblings*. This comparison is faulty because you cannot compare a book to people. You can fix this error by changing *siblings* to *siblings' novels* or *siblings'*, so the comparison pits books against books.

14. **(B)**   *Tense*

This sentence has a tense problem. You know that the action of the sentence is supposed to take place in the past, since the sentence begins with the phrase *over the past ten years*. The main part of the sentence, though, is in the future tense: she *will have achieved* great success. Change the future tense *will have achieved* to the past tense *has achieved*.

15. **(B)** *Pronoun Case*

When you compare a pronoun to a noun, the pronoun must be in the same case as the noun. This sentence compares the *explorers* to the pronoun *him*: *no one among the explorers was more disappointed than him.* The pronoun in this sentence is in the wrong case, since it's being compared to the subject of the sentence, *no one among the explorers.* To fix this error, you should change *him* to *he.*

You can always figure out the correct pronoun case by completing the sentence. A sentence like *Tom is stronger than Joe* is really an abbreviated version of *Tom is stronger than Joe is.* In the abbreviated version, the final verb, *is,* is implied. You can test the correctness of *no one among the explorers was more disappointed than him* by adding the verb *was*: *no one among the explorers was more disappointed than him was.* Since *him was* is grammatically incorrect, you know that *him* is the wrong pronoun case. *He was* is the correct phrase, so you should replace *him* with *he*: *no one among the explorers was more disappointed than he (was).*

16. **(D)** *Subject-Verb Agreement*

Neither is one of those pesky nouns that sound plural but are really singular. Singular nouns must be followed by singular verbs, but in this sentence the singular *neither* is followed by the plural verb *were.* You can correct the sentence by changing *were* to the singular *was.* This subject-verb agreement error is particularly difficult to spot because of the prepositional phrase, *of the scientist's proofs,* separating the subject from the verb. You need to remember to block out confusing prepositional phrases when you're checking for subject-verb agreement.

17. **(D)** *Number Agreement*

Number agreement errors are hard to spot because people make these kinds of errors all the time in speech. The sentence implies that Mary and Bob are going to wear the same coat, but your sense of logic should tell you that they'll each wear a different coat. To correct this error, you should rewrite the sentence to say that they *decided to put on their coats.*

18. **(D)** *Parallelism*

When you see a list on the SAT II Writing, you should look out for parallelism errors. In this list, you have two words that end in *-ing* (*walking* and *living*) followed by *have to eat.* In order to make this list parallel, you need to change *have to eat* into *-ing* form: *eating nothing but canned fish.*

19. **(C)** *Idiom*

In English, people argue *with* other people (*Jim argued with Julie*), and they argue *against* ideas and actions (*Jim argued against going to the movie*). This sentence should say that the girl argued *with* the principal, not *against* him.

20. **(A)** *Tense*

This sentence contains a tricky tense error. *Tear* is one of those verbs with annoying tenses that you just need to memorize: I *tear* (present tense); I *tore* (past tense); I *had torn* (past participle). The verb *had tore* in this sentence is wrong. In order to fix this error, you need to change *tore* to *torn*: *the boy had torn.*

Improving Sentence Errors

21. (C)   *Parallelism*

The original sentence makes a parallelism error when it says that Hubble's function is a verb infinitive (*to locate*) and a gerund (*photographing*). In order to have a parallel sentence, you must state these two verbs in the same form. Choice (C) fixes the error by changing both verbs into gerunds (words that end in -*ing*): *locating and photographing*.

22. (C)   *Coordination*

Bad coordination makes the original sentence sound awkward and wordy. The sentence wants to say that the new equipment allowed the museum to do two things: *to restore the painting* and *to fix the chip on the sculpture*. Don't beat around the bush by saying *and it was also able*. The clearest and simplest way to get the sentence's meaning across is to say *the new conservation equipment enabled the museum to restore the damaged painting and to fix the chip on the sculpture by Bernini*.

23. (E)   *Passive Voice*

You should take every opportunity to get rid of the passive voice (as long as you end up with a grammatically correct sentence). This sentence uses the passive voice twice: the construction *had been supported* by the board, and it *was realized* by the superintendent. Choice (E) rewrites both verbs in the active voice: the board *had supported* the construction, and the superintendent *realized* that the school didn't have enough funds.

Because (E) changes everything in the sentence to the active voice, it is a better answer than (C) or (D). Choices (C) and (D) each fix half of the sentence but leave the other half in the passive voice. (C) leaves the first half of the sentence in the passive voice (*the construction had been supported*), and (D) leaves the second half of the sentence in the passive voice (*it was realized by the superintendent*).

24. (C)   *Parallelism*

The list in the original sentence suffers from faulty parallelism. Since the first two items in the list are noun phrases (*memory loss* and *poor concentration*), the third item must also be a noun. In the original sentence, though, the third item is a verb phrase: *are unable to control their impulses*. Choices (C), (D), and (E) change this verb phrase into a noun phrase, *an inability to control their impulses*, but (D) and (E) commit other grammatical errors. Choice (D) incorrectly modifies the plural noun *people* with the singular pronoun *his or her*, and choice (E) incorrectly replaces *to control* with *of controlling*. Choice (C) is the right answer because it fixes the parallelism error and uses correct grammar.

25. (B)   *Run-on*

The original sentence is a run-on. Two independent clauses (*seats are still available on the afternoon train* and *you can purchase your ticket at the station*) are crammed together without any punctuation dividing them. Choice (B) is the best answer because it joins the two clauses with a semicolon. Choice (C), like the original sentence, is a run-on because a comma isn't strong enough to join together independent clauses without a conjunction (such as *and*, *but*, or *for*). Choice (D) is wrong because it changes the sentence to say that seats are still available at the station, and choice (E) is wrong because it uses the passive voice in the second half of the sentence.

26. **(D)** *Fragment*

In order for a sentence to be complete, it must contain an independent clause—a clause capable of being a sentence on its own. The original sentence in this question lacks an independent clause. Instead, it has two dependent clauses: *after the media vilified him* and *booing and jeering the man wherever he went*. Choice (D) fixes this sentence fragment by changing *booing and jeering the man* into an independent clause with a subject and verb: *the man was booed and jeered*. Although choice (C) also makes this change, it adds the unnecessary conjunction *but*.

27. **(C)** *Misplaced Modifier*

The original sentence incorrectly places the modifier *like many neophytes in the business world* next to the noun phrase *the discovery of the depths*, thus implying that the discovery is the neophyte. What the sentence really wants to say is that the man (*him*) is the neophyte in the business world. Choice (C) fixes this error by rephrasing the sentence so that the man is next to his modifier: *like many neophytes, he was shocked*. Although (D) and (E) also place the modifier correctly, they make other grammatical errors. Choice (D) makes a pronoun error when it modifies the plural noun *rivals* with the singular pronoun *his or her*, and choice (E) uses an incorrect verb tense: *to have maintained*.

28. **(B)** *Parallelism*

The problem with this sentence is the faulty parallelism in the list. The first two items in the list are noun phrases (*miniature sound receiver* and *amplifier*), but the third item is a verb phrase (*to transfer the amplified sound by either an earpiece or a vibrator*). Choice (B) fixes the parallelism error by turning the third item into the noun phrase *either an earpiece or a vibrator to transfer the amplified sound*.

29. **(A)** *No Error*

No error.

30. **(B)** *Tense*

The first verb in the sentence, *to have had the opportunity*, tells you that the sentence's action takes place in the past, but the second verb is in the future tense: *will have to get*. In order to fix this tense error, you should put the second verb in the past tense: *would have had to have gotten*.

31. **(E)** *Subject-Verb Agreement*

None is a singular noun and requires a singular verb, so you need to change the plural *were* to the singular *was*. Both choices (D) and (E) make this change, but (E) is the better answer because (D) uses an awkward, wordy structure.

32. **(C)** *Faulty Comparison*

The faulty comparison in this sentence will be hard to catch because your ear may gloss over the error. The sentence wants to compare the advantages of a secure job to the advantages of a creative job, but it ends up comparing these advantages to the creative job itself. Choice (C) corrects this faulty parallelism by rewriting the sentence as *Some people point to the advantages of a job offering security over the advantages of a job offering creative fulfillment.*

33. **(D)** *Subject-Verb Agreement*

In *neither/nor* constructions the verb should agree with the noun following *nor*. In this sentence, *nor* is followed by the plural noun phrase *the bride's brothers*, so the verb in the sentence must also be plural. In order to correct this subject-verb agreement error, you need to change the singular verb *was* to the plural *were*. Choices (C), (D), and (E) make this change, but (C) uses an incorrect verb tense (*were disapproving*) and (E) has bad coordination (*the wedding, and the siblings disapproved of it*). Choice (D) is the best answer.

34. **(A)** *No Error*

No error.

35. **(D)** *Coordination*

The original sentences uses poor coordination. You can express the relationship between the two clauses— *Evelyn Waugh wrote novels* and *they satirize upper-class English society*—by making the second clause dependent on the first. Choice (D) rewrites the original sentence as: *Evelyn Waugh wrote novels that satirize upper-class English society.* (D) creates a clear and concise sentence, making it the best of the answer choices.

36. **(A)** *No Error*

No error.

37. **(C)** *Misplaced Modifier*

The way the original sentence is written implies that Olivia's missing flute was walking by the kitchen table. Since flutes don't usually walk, you can fairly assume the sentence wants to say that while Olivia was walking by the table, she found her flute. Choice (C) is the best revision of the sentence, since it states that Olivia was the one who did the walking.

38. **(A)** *No Error*

No error.

Improving Paragraphs

39. **(D)** *Revision*

The original sentence is redundant. Because *even though* and *however* serve the same function in the sentence (they describe a contrast), you should use only one of them. Choice (D) gets rid of *however*, forming a sentence that begins with a dependent clause (*Even though some people . . .*) and ends with an independent clause (*I think it is . . .*). Choice (D) also gets rid of the wordiness in the last part of the sentence by changing *the most enjoyable of all the spectator sports* to *the most enjoyable spectator sport*. Although choice (E) gets rid of *even though*, it changes the meaning of the sentence by putting *however* before *some people think it's boring*.

40. **(A)**   *Combining Sentences*

In order to answer combination questions, you need to understand the relationship between the two sentences. Sentence 4 says that *some of my friends say that baseball is boring*, and sentence 5 says that *the game seems slow*. First ask yourself who thinks the game is slow: the writer or the writer's friends? Since the writer has already expressed enthusiasm for the game, you can bet that his friends are the ones who find it slow. Now you need to relate sentence 5 to sentence 4. One logical connection is that the friends think baseball is boring *because* it seems slow. Choice (A) makes this connection: *Some of my friends say that baseball is boring because the game seems slow.*

You can check your answer by running through the other choices. Choice (B) replaces the period between the two sentences with a semicolon. Although the resulting sentence is grammatically correct, it does nothing to explain the relationship between the two sentences. *But* in (C) and *despite this* in (D) incorrectly contrast the two sentences. (E) creates a sentence fragment by linking the two sentences with a comma.

41. **(B)**   *Addition*

The first thing you should do when tackling an addition question is read what comes immediately before and immediately after the addition. In this case, the addition follows two sentences that say baseball is boring and slow, and it begins a sentence that says baseball's slow pace is what makes it great. Sentence 6, which gives the writer's opinion, is in contrast to sentences 4 and 5, which give the friends' opinion. Since you're looking for a phrase that describes a contrast, you can rule out choices (A) and (E). You can also rule out choice (D), since it creates a sentence with a misplaced modifier. Choice (C) points to a contrast, but it doesn't make much sense in the context of the paragraph. The contrast seems to be in the pace of the game rather than in the opinions of the writer and his friends. Choice (B) is the best answer because it clearly states that sentence 6, unlike sentences 4 and 5, represents the writer's opinion.

42. **(D)**   *Revision*

The original sentence has two pronoun errors: a pronoun shift and a pronoun agreement error. The sentence shifts from addressing the pronoun *you* to addressing the pronoun *one*, even though *you* and *one* refer to the same person, the reader. In order to correct this mistake, you need to change *one* to *you*. Both (D) and (E) make this change, but (E) fails to correct the pronoun agreement error in *its players*. In the original sentence, the singular possessive pronoun *its* incorrectly takes the place of the plural possessive noun *managers'* (as in the *managers' players*). In order to make the possessive pronoun agree wtih its plural antecedent, you need to change *its* to *their*. Choice (D) is the correct answer because it fixes both of these errors.

43. **(B)**   *Addition*

The best answer will serve as a transition from the second paragraph and as a topic sentence for the third. The second paragraph ends by telling you to watch the dugout when nothing seems to be happening on the field. The third paragraph tells you about other amusing things you can do at the baseball park. Choice (B) is the best sentence because it says that *baseball offers many other diversions* in addition to what's happening in the game. Choice (E) has a similar meaning, but it is wordy and uses the passive voice.

44. **(C)**   *Analysis*

The easiest way to answer this question is to go through the answer choices, ruling out the ones that the writer *does* do. The writer does present an argument, which says that baseball is fun. The author tells you an opposing viewpoint: baseball is boring. Sentence 9 describes a hypothetical situation in which nothing happens on the baseball field, and in the last paragraph, the writer relates an anecdote about his attempt to throw a strike. The writer does not do choice (C), debunking a popular belief.

45. (E)   *Revision*

The main problem with the original sentence is a pronoun agreement error. In the sentence, the plural pronoun *their* modifies the singular pronoun *everyone*. In order to fix this error, you should change *their* to the singular *his or her*. Both (D) and (E) make this change, but (D) commits a subject-verb agreement error when it says that *everyone know*. Since *everyone* is singular, it must be followed by the singular verb *knows* instead of the plural *know*.

46. (B)   *Analysis*

When answering an analysis question like this one, you should try to come up with your own answer before looking at the answer choices. Quickly reread the introduction, and decide what purpose sentence 4 serves in it. In sentence 3, the writer says that everything we know is subjective. Then he asks the question, *how can we know whether what I perceive to be the color red is the same as what you perceive to be red?* The purpose of this question is to illustrate the impossibility of knowing someone else's viewpoint, since you can know only your own viewpoint. Choice (B), which says that the sentence is *an example of the problem of subjectivity*, is the correct answer. You may be tempted to choose (C) because it says that sentence 4 is a question, but sentence 4 is not a question that the writer tries to answer. In fact, the writer says that we'll probably *never know the answer* to it.

47. (C)   *Addition*

The vague word *this* refers to the question asked in sentence 4. You can make sentence 5 more precise by adding the word *question*: *we'll never know the answer to this question.*

48. (E)   *Revision*

Sentence 8 has a misplaced modifier. Since *the realization* directly follows *watching this show*, the sentence implies that the realization watched television. What the sentence really wants to say is that the writer watched the show, so you need to move the pronoun *I* next to the phrase *watching this show*. Choices (D) and (E) fix the misplaced modifier, but (E) is the better answer because (D) uses the passive voice.

49. (B)   *Combining Sentences*

This question asks you to perform two tasks: revise and combine. First figure out the logical way to combine the two sentences. The first sentence says that the protagonist lost his feet, and the second one says that he could still feel them, so you know that the second sentence is in contrast to the first. You can rule out choice (C), since it connects the two sentences with the conjunction *and*, which doesn't express contrast. You can also rule out choice (E), since it also fails to express contrast. Of the remaining answer choices, (B) is the best. It uses the conjunction *but* to establish the contrast, and it fixes the verb tense error in the second sentence by changing the past tense *imagined* to the present tense *imagines*. Neither (A) nor (D) fixes this tense error, because their sentences illogically shift from the present tense (*loses* and *can still feel*) to the past (*imagined*).

50. (B)   *Revision*

In sentence 12, the pronoun *they* is ambiguous. Three plural nouns precede it, so you need to specify the one to which it refers: *amputees*, *limbs*, or *sensations*. In the context of the sentence, *they* most likely refers to the *missing limbs*, especially since the sentence says the amputees think *they are still there*, suggesting *they* are now gone. You can improve the sentence by replacing *they* with *these limbs*, choice (B): *amputees often sense in their missing limbs physical sensations and are convinced that these limbs are still there.*

Identifying Sentence Errors

51. **(D)** *Wrong Word*

Unintelligent, which means stupid, is the wrong word in this context. *Unintelligible*, which means not comprehended or not understood, makes more sense than *unintelligent*. The sentence suggests that Benedict couldn't hear the conversation next door, since he strained to listen through the thick walls; in other words, the conversation was unintelligible, since he could not hear it.

52. **(A)** *Adverb*

This sentence incorrectly uses the adjective *graceful* to describe how the horse jumped. Verbs, such as *jumped*, should be modified by adverbs, not adjectives. To correct this error, you should change *graceful* to the adverb *gracefully*.

53. **(B)** *Double Negative*

Not scarcely is a classic double negative. Since double negatives cancel out, the sentence actually says that there *was* snow falling. Whenever you see words like *scarcely, barely, hardly*, or *not*, you should look out for illegal double negatives.

54. **(B)** *Ambiguous Pronoun*

If you read through this sentence quickly, you may not notice any problems with it. The sentence is grammatically correct, but it uses an ambiguous pronoun, *they*, which doesn't refer to any noun in the sentence. On first reading, you may think that *they* refers to the plural noun *protesters*, but the sentence wouldn't make much sense if that were true. Most likely, *they* refers to reporters writing about the protest, but you can't be sure that this is true. Because you can't say for certain what *they* modifies, *they* is an ambiguous pronoun.

55. **(E)** *No Error*

No error.

56. **(C)** *Pronoun Agreement*

Team is a singular noun, so the pronoun that modifies it should also be singular. In this sentence, though, it is modified by a plural pronoun, *their*. Fix this error by replacing *their* with *its*.

57. **(A)** *Idiom*

In English, the expression is *in accordance with*, not *in accordance in*. Idiomatic errors involving pronouns are often easy to catch with your ear, since the errors will often sound strange to you.

58. **(D)** *Wrong Word*

Credulous means gullible, while *credible* means believable. *Credible* is the right word in this context, since the prosecutor is complaining about the reliability of a defense witness. A prosecutor is more likely to complain that a witness is not believable than to complain that a witness is not gullible.

59. **(B)**   *Comparative Modifier*

Many people use *fewer* and *less* interchangeably, but the two words have distinct uses. You should apply *fewer* to things you can count: months, hours, people, and peas, for instance. You should apply *less* to things you can't count, like rain, time, and love. Since you can count the number of distractions in the classroom, you should replace *less* in this sentence with *fewer*.

60. **(E)**   *No Error*

No error.